Ca Contributions:

SOCIOLOGY AND POLICY

Andrew Greeley

William McManus

THE THOMAS MORE PRESS
Chicago, Illinois

ANDREW M. GREELEY
is Professor of Sociology
at the University of Arizona.

WILLIAM E. McMANUS
is retired Bishop of
Fort Wayne-South Bend, IN.

Copyright © 1987 by Andrew M. Greeley and
William E. McManus. All rights reserved. Printed in
the United States of America. No part of this
publication may be reproduced, stored in a retrieval
system, transmitted in any form or by any means,
electronic, mechanical, photocopying, recording or
otherwise, without the written permission of the
publisher, The Thomas More Association, 223 West
Erie Street, Chicago, Illinois 60610.

ISBN 0-88347-216-3

A SOCIOLOGIST'S

REPORT

Andrew Greeley

1.1 / OVERVIEW

Although American Catholics earn, on the average, over a thousand dollars a year more than their Protestant counterparts, Catholics' financial contributions to their church are much less than those of Protestants: on the average, three hundred and twenty dollars a year as opposed to five hundred and eighty dollars a year for American Protestants. Catholics contribute 1.1% of their income to the church while Protestants give 2.2% of their income to the church.

This difference cannot be attributed to any failings of charity or generosity among Catholics, who on measures of attitude and behavior are at least as generous as Protestants. Nor can it be explained as a result of "inflation" because inflation affects all Americans. Nor is it caused by Catholic schools or by larger Catholic families. Those who send their children to Catholic schools contribute more rather than less to the Church than do other Catholics; and the greatest differences between Protestants and Catholics occur among those who have two children or less.

Nor can the difference be accounted for by changing levels of Catholic church attendance. If all Catholics went to Mass every week and contributed as much to the Church as those who presently go every week, their contributions would still be less than those of their Protestant counterparts. Nor is the lower level of Catholic contributions the result of better-organized Protestant fund-raising in which fixed pledges are fulfilled every year.

This difference between Protestants and Catholics in financial support of their churches persists in every demographic, social, and economic group--young and old, affluent and less affluent, white collar and blue collar, college educated and not college educated, and between Catholics and all Protestant denominational groupings. It also is independent of their perceptions of their disposable income.

Moreover, the present situation is the result of a dramatic change in patterns of contribution to one's church over the last twenty-five years. In the early nineteen sixties, Catholics gave the same proportion of their income to their church as did Protestants. In the last quarter century, the Protestant contribution rate has remained stable at approximately two percent of annual income while the Catholic rate has fallen from more than two percent to about one percent.

This decline cannot be explained by the decline in Sunday church attendance (which stopped in 1975 while the decline in financial contributions has continued) nor by the costs of Catholic education nor by inflation nor by opposition to the Second Vatican Council. Some of the change (about a fifth) is the result of the influx of a younger generation of Catholics who contribute less to the Church than do their Protestant youthful counterparts. More of the change (about a half) can be attributed to changing Catholic attitudes on sex and authority in their church.

It is therefore suggested that the decline in Catholic contributions over the last quarter century is the result of a failure in leadership and an alienation of membership, not from the Catholic community or from sacramental participation but from support of the ecclesiastical institution.

Thus, any of the reforms in Catholic fundraising currently proposed are likely to have only small success, at best, if there is not some fundamental restructuring of the relation between leaders and members. In the present situation, attempts to impose "tithing"--whatever that might mean--are likely to be counterproductive.

The financial losses to the Catholic Church of this decline in contributions are dramatic. If Catholics contributed not a tenth, not even a fifth of their income to the Church, but only the same 2.2% of their income that Protestants do, American Catholicism would have available almost twice the annual funds that it currently has--six billion more dollars to maintain Catholic schools, to pay employees more than poverty wages, to continue to maintain its inner-city ministry, to found new parishes, and to do something more than talk about an "option for the poor."

1.2 / PRELIMINARIES

This book is the result of a conversation between William McManus and Andrew Greeley that occurred in Tucson during the winter of 1986. The issue of Catholic financial contributions was in the air for a number of different reasons.

A reaction had set in to the pastoral letter of the American bishops on poverty (*Economic Justice for All: Catholic Social Teaching and the U.S. Economy*). How, it was being asked, could the bishops denounce poverty and still pay poverty wages to their own employees? While the pastoral was revised to take into account the obligations of the Church itself to pay appropriate wages to those who worked for it, there was no visible change in the salaries of church workers and no reason to believe that the words of the pastoral would cause such a change.

Bishop McManus's article in *America*, "Putting Our Own House in Order," stirred up some criticism. The Church, he was told, could not afford reforms of the sort he demanded. This response led some observers to note that it was the same excuse that everyone else used for paying substandard wages and that those who used it were in a poor position to offer moral advice to others.

The well-publicized pastoral letter on nuclear weapons involved no financial costs for the bishops who signed it. The equally well-publicized pastoral on poverty, however, put the bishops in the awkward position where they will have to pay a very large cost to avoid the challenge that they are not practicing what they preach, a position that was apparently not anticipated when the earlier drafts of the pastoral were enthusiastically approved.

At the same time, the long battle over Catholic schools continued. The Church, it was said, could no longer afford to maintain a private school system. Or at least it could not afford both white suburban schools and black and hispanic inner-city schools. Bishop McManus was scheduled to make a presentation on the subject to the annual meeting of the National Catholic Educational Association and sought data from me on Catholic financial contributions in comparison with Protestant financial contributions.

While my colleagues and I had reported on Catholic financial contributions from 1963 to 1974 in our *Catholic Schools in a Declining Church* (1976), the data at that time had not allowed us to compare Catholic and Protestant financial contributions. We were told that the erosion of Catholic contributions we reported was typical of all religious denominations. Moreover, our chapter on church finances was largely ignored in the controversy over other chapters on changing sexual attitudes. We were able to settle the argument that Catholic contributions were lower because of the burden on some families of Catholic school tuition. In fact, on the average, those with children in Catholic schools contributed *more* to the Church (in addition to their school tuition) than did those with no children in Catholic schools, enough more to account for whatever subsidies on the national average were necessary to support the Catholic schools.

(As we shall see in this report, Catholic school parents also contribute more than Protestants do to their churches. If everyone gave at the level of Catholic school parents, the per capita contributions of Catholics would far exceed the per capita contributions of Protestants.)

That finding apparently went unnoticed, even by such a sympathetic observer as Bishop McManus, who raised it again with me in our conversations in the winter of 1986. The conviction that tuition costs in Catholic schools explain the problems of Sunday collections is so much part of the conventional wisdom of the Catholic clergy and hierarchy that it is inconceivable that it not be true. Clear and conclusive findings that reject such an explanation are treated as though they do not exist.

The bishop also asked me if it was indeed certain that Catholics now earn as much money as Protestants. I replied that it was as certain as anything can be in the world of survey analysis that Catholics now earn *more* money than Protestants, particularly if the Catholics happen to be Irish or Italian. Yet the persistence of the Immigration /Depression myth among priests and bishops is still so strong that the explanation "our people can't afford it"--rarely used in the actual Immigration/Depression era by the way--is still heard and accepted. As will be demonstrated in this report, "our people," without making any more sacrifices than our Protestant brothers and sisters, could afford twice the contributions they are now making.

In the long argument about the costs of Catholic schools, no one, as far as I know, has seriously raised the issue of how a church made up of mostly working-class immigrants and the children of immigrants could afford a comprehensive

Catholic school system while a church with a large proportion of college-educated professionals cannot afford such a school system.

The bishop recalled the days of Cardinal Meyer in the late nineteen fifties and early nineteen sixties when the Archdiocese of Chicago raised twenty million dollars for new high schools. Such fund-raising, he thought, would be impossible today. Yet the reason for the change was not clear. I pointed out to him that the high school education in Catholic schools of two young people costs about sixteen thousand dollars, as much as a new, top-of-the-line Buick. In 1940, a similar Catholic secondary education would have cost about twelve hundred dollars, also the price of a top-of-the-line Buick.

Catholic schools continued to be closed around the country, almost always because of the decisions of bishops and priests and nuns and usually in the face of opposition from the laity.

Lay support for Catholic schools, in principle and in theory, had not changed. Comparative costs had not changed. What had changed?

That, of course, was the question that Bishop McManus was addressing to me--no small problem on a warm winter afternoon in the Santa Catalina mountains.

The only data then available, as far as I knew, were from a recent Gallup survey. The finding, as reported in the press, was scary: Protestants and Jews were twice as likely (twenty percent as opposed to ten percent) to give more than five hundred dollars a year to their church. I promised the bishop that I would try to search out data that would be useful for his NCEA talk and from which we might be able to piece together a joint effort like this volume.

Subsequently, other events, about which we talked on the phone, increased interest in the subject matter. Bishops and priests around the country, hard-pressed to pay their bills, began to talk about a system of "tithing" to meet the skyrocketing costs of their parishes and schools--providing a solution, as humans are wont, before they knew the nature of the problem.

In Chicago, the Cardinal announced that bingo would be discontinued as a means of fundraising and promised a new system of Catholic finance, the details of which were not explained. Protests from the parishes did not make the press but were loud on the clerical grapevine. At the same time, several affluent suburban parishes had, in the year or two after the appointment of a new pastor, exhausted their reserves and were running on large deficits. The pastors had adopted the counterproductive strategy of preaching, to hear the laity tell it, about nothing but money.

What had happened to Catholic contributions, not since the late thirties and early forties, but in a more recent time frame--since, let us say, the period of Bishop McManus's high school fund drive in the late fifties and early sixties?

The answer, to anticipate briefly the findings of this report, is that there has been a catastrophic-- I used the word advisedly--decline in the annual contributions of American Catholics to their church. From being as generous as Protestants a quarter of a century ago, Catholics are now only half as generous.

I did not expect this sort of finding that afternoon on the outskirts of Tucson. I knew from our 1976 report on the 1963 and 1974 studies of American Catholics that Catholic contributions, as a proportion of income, had fallen. I had seen hints that Catholics gave less to their religious institution than did either Protestants or Jews. But I would have underestimated both the steepness of the decline and the magnitude of the difference. The use of the word "catastrophic" was forced on me by the data.

Shortly after Bishop McManus returned from Tucson to Mount Prospect, I read in the papers of a study entitled *The Charitable Behavior of Americans*, executed in 1984 by the Yankelovich organization for the Washington-based Independent Sector with a grant from the Rockefeller Brothers Fund. The finding that leaped out of the press accounts is that reported in the first paragraph of the "Overview" of this report: Catholics give only about half as much to their church as do Protestants.

The authors of the report did not analyze the religious differences because such an analysis was not part of their mandate, but it appeared from the press accounts and a later reading of the report that there might be raw materials in the project for a serious and detailed study of current Catholic financial contributions.

I deputed my research assistant, Sean Durkin, to find out if the data were available for analysis. Indeed they were, at the moment the Independent Sector report was released.   Sean

Durkin, with the assistance of (people at Independent Sector and NORC and anyone else who ought to be acknowledged), prepared the data for analysis on the SPSSPC+ system of desk-top data analysis. I will begin the data reporting in the next chapter with an analysis of the Independent Sector data both because that is how this project began and because, with this particular problem, it seems better to describe the present situation in some detail first and then reach back into the past to ascertain whether what we observe today about Catholic contributions has ever been thus.

We had available the 1974 and 1963 National Opinion Research Center (NORC) studies of American Catholics, so we could make estimates of the changes in Catholic contributions over twenty years (although the primary focus of both these studies was educational and not financial). However, we needed other data both to confirm the NORC findings and to measure the trends in Protestant contributions. (The NORC studies were confined to Catholics.)

With the assistance of Tom Smith of NORC's General Social Survey, Sean Durkin uncovered two studies that seemed to be appropriate, both done at the University of Michigan's Survey Research Center, one in 1974 and the other in 1960. In addition a 1982 study provided confirmation in the nineteen eighties of the Yankelovich project.

All six data sets are based on probability samples. The NORC and SRC studies were executed through personal interviews; the Yankelovich project was carried out by telephone interviews.

The number of cases in each of the studies was as follows:

SRC 1960 = 2997
SRC 1975 = 2802
NORC 1963 = 2071
NORC 1974 = 940
Gallup 1982 = 1411
Yankelovich 1984 = 1151.
Total = 10,672

The two principle findings of this report are both statistically significant at very high levels of confidence: Catholics give less than Protestants and this lesser contribution is the result of long-term decline in proportion of income given to the Church.

The strategy of this analysis may seem patchwork: six different studies with different foci and from different organizations, not explicitly designed to address the problem under consideration. While the findings presented in this section of the book are no substitute for a full-scale study of Catholic contributions (a study that would be as wise a result of this analysis as it is an unlikely result), the strategy utilized is nothing of which one need be ashamed. Science searches for evidence wherever it can find it. Moreover, the NORC and SRC studies confirm and validate one another, far more closely than statistical requirements would necessitate. Finally, the 1984 Yankelovich survey produced similar proportions of income given to the respective churches by Protestants and Catholics in the 1982 Gallup study. Thus in three of the four studies in which Protesetants are sampled the proportion of income given to their churches is 2.2% and in one (Gallup / 1982) the proportion is 2.1%. In both studies in the early sixties the Catholic proportion is 2.2%. In the two studies in middle seventies the Catholic proportion has declined to 1.6% and in both studies in the eighties the Catholic proportion is 1.1%. Not only are the key findings in this report based on more than ten thousand respondents they are also based on six separate studies conducted by four different research organizations, each with their own independent sample frame.

Thus, while there are imperfections in this approach, as in all scientific efforts, the data supporting my two major findings are better than one can expect to obtain in most longitudinal research analyses. Most sociologists who pursue the craft of survey data analysis would advise the reader that no reasonable person should doubt either of the two principle findings.

All the data are on the public record should anyone else wish to analyze them. Indeed, I would be happy to share my SPSSPC+ diskettes with any scholar who wishes to work with them.

The notion of using financial contributions as a "religious indicator" has not hitherto been advanced in the sociology of religion subprofession, which shows perhaps what an ivory-tower world we who work in the field must live in. It is obviously a very useful measure because it taps the "put your money where your mouth is" dimension of religion, the willingness of a believer to make some financial sacrifices for his/her beliefs. Moreover, as this report indicates, it is a measure that, while it correlates with other more traditional measures such as church attendance, can fluctuate independently of them: Catholic church attendance has not declined since 1975; Catholic financial contributions have continued to decline.

It is thus a measure of religious behavior which can distinguish between loyalty to a religious heritage and ritual practice on the one hand and acceptance of the legitimacy of institutional leadership on the other. The possible separation of these two dimensions of religion is, from the viewpoint of social science, the most interesting and the most unexpected aspect of the changes in American Catholicism over the past twenty-five years.

It is also a phenomenon for which Catholic leadership was unprepared and which it still in great part will not accept or acknowledge.

Nor have there been any efforts, as far as I know, to compare in any detail the differences in financial contributions of Protestants and Catholics and the changes in these differences over time. Thus, the present report breaks new ground not out of ambition but out of necessity. There are no theories to test because there has never been speculation on the subject.

God and the NORC advisory board willing, I hope to include periodically in the NORC General Social Survey a question about financial contributions to one's denomination so that changes in this measure over time can be observed and so that others may, if they wish, replicate the findings of this report in years to come.

The next chapter will present the findings of my research on the 1984 study. The subsequent chapter will reach back into the past and see what changes have occurred in Protestant and Catholic financial contributions in the last quarter century. I shall then turn to a search for an explanation of the catastrophic decline in Catholic contributions since the early nineteen sixties. Finally, I will attempt to interpret the meaning of my findings, speculate about their implications, and offer some tentative recommendations--much more personal and much less certain enterprises then data presentation.

1.3 / THE PRESENT

In **1984**, the typical American Catholic gave three hundred and twenty dollars to his/her church; the typical Protestant gave five hundred and eighty dollars. This two hundred-sixty-dollar advantage of Protestants over Catholics in church contributions exists despite the fact that the average Catholic earned $27,500 and the typical Protestant earned $26,400. The Catholic contribution as proportion of income was 1.2% of income, and the typical Protestant gave 2.2%. If the Catholic rate was also 2.2%, the average Catholic contribution would be six hundred and five dollars.

There are some eighty-five million families and unrelated individuals in the United States. Catholics are about one quarter of the American population; thus, there are approximately twenty-one million Catholic families and unrelated individuals.

If Catholics were giving 2.2% of their income to the Church, the annual income of the Catholic Church would be 12.7 billion dollars, as opposed to six billion in the present circumstances. Thus, the Catholic Church is "losing" approximately six billion dollars in income that it might have if its people were as generous with their income as are Protestants.

This statement is not opinion or guesswork or an estimate. Rather, it is the result of simple multiplication and subtraction: $320 times 21 million equals $6.72 billion; $605 times 21 million equals $12.71 billion; and $12.71 billion minus $6.72 billion equals $5.99 billion.

With that much extra money, American Catholicism would be able to maintain its inner-city schools in service of blacks and hispanics; pay more than poverty wages to its employees (and thus honor the "preferential option for the poor" about which its leadership talks so much); open new schools in its suburban parishes; do serious research on its principal problems, including the shortage of vocations to the priesthood and the religious life; and contribute to the support of the Church and of human dignity in the poor countries of the world.

The crucial question, then, is why Catholics are so much less generous to their church than are Protestants.

Indeed, they are less generous than members of all Protestant denominations. Every Protestant denomination receives more than 2.0% of their constituents' income, except the Methodists and Lutherans who receive 1.7% of the income of their members.

How can one explain this striking discrepancy in generosity to one's church?

Are Catholics inherently less generous than Protestants?

The evidence is mixed, but it would appear that the absence of generosity is not a primary explanation. Catholics give one hundred and forty dollars a year to "non-religious" charities--somewhat less than Protestant contribution of one hundred and eighty dollars a year, but the difference is not statistically significant (0.5% versus 0.7% of income).

On a wide variety of attitudes towards the use of money for welfare purposes, there are either no differences between Catholics and Protestants or the differences are not statistically significant or Catholics report more generous attitudes than do Protestants.

Thus, eighty-three percent of American Catholics believe that the government has an obligation to care for the needy, as opposed to seventy-three percent of Protestants. Seventy percent of Catholics reject the notion that the government is giving too much to the poor, in comparison with sixty-three percent of the Protestants. Thirty-seven percent of Catholics, as against twenty-seven percent of Protestants, reject the proposition that it is better to help the poor in your own communities than to help people elsewhere. Forty-three percent of Catholics, as opposed to thirty-six percent of Protestants, disagree with the notion that the government should not help the poor in the less developed countries. On all four of these attitudes, the differences between members of the two denominations are statistically significant.

A little more than half of both groups say that they give about as much as do others and only a sixth say that they give less--judgments that in the case of Catholics are not accurate because in fact they give much less than do their Protestant fellow Americans. Fifty-six percent of Protestants and Catholics alike say that they should give more to charity.

If they "should" give more money to charities (all charities and not just religious), why don't they?

There are almost no differences in the Catholic and Protestant responses to this question.

Two thirds of both groups say that they cannot afford to. A little under thirty percent say that they would rather spend the money in other ways. Only five percent say that the charities do not deserve support. Fourteen percent report that no one had asked them to make a contribution, and a quarter say that they did not get around to making a contribution. (The total adds to more than one hundred percent because multiple responses were possible.)

Finally, two thirds of both denominations say that they worry about money in the future, but only a little more than a fifth of each group say that they worry "a lot" about money in the future.

Thus, in the items used in the Independent Sector study (data from which are the basis for this chapter), there is little evidence that Catholics are inherently less generous than Protestants. An answer to the problem of why they then give so much less to their church must be found in the nature of the relationship between Catholics and their ecclesiastical institution.

Two of the explanations often given for the impression that Catholics give less is that they have larger families and that the costs of Catholic schools explain the lower contributions of Catholics: money that would otherwise be given to the Church is diverted to meet the demands for Catholic school tuition.

While Catholic families are still somewhat larger than Protestant families, that fact does not account for the differences between the two communities in religious giving: Protestants with no children give four hundred and six dollars a year more than Catholics; Protestants with one child give one hundred and fifty-one more dollars, with two children one hundred and ninety more dollars, and with three or more children four hundred and sixty-seven more dollars (see *Figure 3.1*). The Protestant advantage exists, then, at every level of family size, especially among those with the largest families and among those who have no children.

Figure 3.1
Annual Contribution
By Denomination and Number of Children

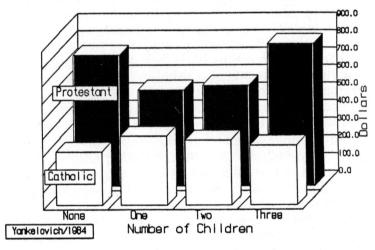

(Some hints on interpreting bar graphs: The black bars always represent Protestant contributions, the white bars Catholic contributions. The horizontal label represents the intervening variable--in this case family size. The vertical bar is the dependent variable--in this case dollars contributed per year. The black bars (dollars contributed by Protestants) are higher than the white bars (dollars contributed by Catholics) at every one of the four levels of family size but especially higher for those with no children and those with three or more children.)

While there was no question in the Independent Sector study about educational costs, there was an item about "disposable" income--the amount you had left after you paid for the basic necessities of life. Catholics were significantly *more* likely to say that they had disposable income: seventy-eight percent of Catholics and seventy-one percent of Protestants reported this excess of income. However, at every level of "disposable" income, Protestants still contributed more to their religion, two hundred dollars among those who said that they had a small amount left over, and five hundred and seventy-two dollars among those who said that they had a moderate amount or a lot left over. Only among those who had just enough money for the basic necessities was there a similarity in contribution--one hundred and fifty-one dollars among Protestants and one hundred and eighty-four dollars among Catholics--virtually the only advantage of contribution that Catholics enjoy in the entire study and one that is not significant statistically (*Figure 3.2*).

Figure 3.2
**Annual Contribution
By Denomination and Disposable Income**

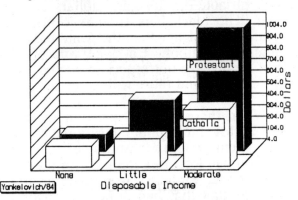

Figure 3.3
**Annual Contribution
By Denomination and Age**

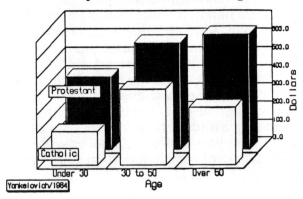

Figure 3.4
Annual Contribution
By Denomination and Education

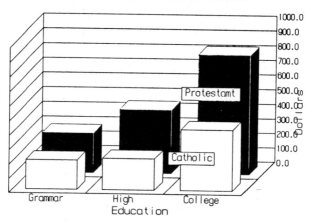

Figure 3.5
Annual Contribution
By Denomination and Income

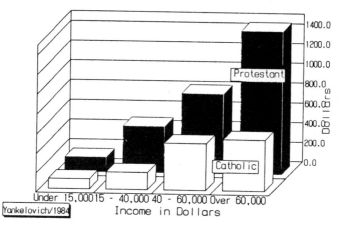

Thus, it is only among the hard-pressed Catholics that generosity comparable to that of Protestant counterparts is found. Among other Americans, Protestants far exceed Catholics in the amount they give to their church. While one cannot say for sure on the basis of these data, it does not seem likely that pressure from Catholic school tuition will be an important factor in accounting for the differences since the biggest differences are among those who report that they have more than "a small amount left over" from the "basic necessities."

How is this "extra" money spent? There is no evidence that Catholics are any more guilty of "materialism" than their Protestant brothers and sisters in the use of this "disposable" income. Sixty-one percent of the Catholic respondents and fifty-seven of the Protestants report that they spend money on savings and investing. Thirty percent of the Catholics and thirty-four percent of the Protestants say that they spend "extra" on vacations; fifty-seven percent of the Catholics and sixty-one percent of the Protestants report that they spend "extra" on buying "nice things"; and sixty-four percent of both groups say that they spend "extra" on helping their friends.

The differences persist in demographic and socio-economic categories. Among those under thirty, Catholics give one hundred and ninety dollars, Protestants four hundred and six dollars; in the thirty to fifty age category, Protestants give five hundred and ninety dollars, Catholics four hundred and twenty-two. Among those over fifty, the contributions are three hundred and twenty for Catholics, six hundred and thirty-seven for Protestants (*Figure 3.3*).

Catholics with professional occupations give four hundred and ten dollars; their Protestant opposites give nine hundred and eighty-three dollars. Blue collar Catholics give two hundred and fifty-four dollars; blue collar Protestants contribute five hundred and fifteen dollars.

Protestants who have attended college average eight hundred and twenty-eight dollars, as opposed to four hundred and twenty-four dollars for their Catholic counterparts. For high school graduates (who did not go to college), the numbers are four hundred and forty-one dollars and two hundred and nineteen dollars. Only at the bottom of the educational ladder--among those who did not graduate from high school--do the contributions converge: two hundred and six dollars for Catholics and two hundred and seventy-six dollars for Protestants (*Figure 3.4*).

Finally, Protestants who earn under fifteen thousand dollars a year give one hundred and fifty dollars a year to their church, forty-seven dollars more than Catholics in that income bracket. In the fifteen to forty thousand dollar category, Protestants donate four hundred and seventy-four dollars, Catholics one hundred and seventy-seven dollars less. The biggest difference is among those who earn more than forty thousand dollars: in the forty to sixty-thousand category, Catholics give four hundred and eighty-one dollars, and Protestants donate three hundred and thirty-three dollars more. Among those who earn more than sixty thousand dollars a year, Catholics give five hundred and twenty-five dollars, Protestants fourteen hundred and fifty-three dollars (*Figure 3.5*).

Thus, in all groups, save among those who are financially hard-pressed, Protestants are more generous to their church than Catholics. Moreover, these differences seem to be especially strong among the better educated and the more affluent. The Catholic families who earn less than fifteen thousand and who did not graduate from high school are the only ones who come within striking distance of Protestants in financial contributions.

The problem of lower Catholic contributions cannot be explained, then, by the fact that Catholics are poorer than Protestants: at the near-poverty levels both groups are about equally generous. The differences are to be found at the middle- and upper-income levels, precisely among those Catholics whose financial and educational success ought to have made them able to match Protestant contributions.

Do Catholics think that their church, for one reason or another, does not deserve more money? This question cannot be answered directly since none of the items in the survey are designed to ask why respondents do not contribute more to their churches. However, the series of questions about why more is not given to charity enables us to approximate an answer. Only about five percent of both denominations were willing to say that the charities did not deserve the money. Among this group, astonishingly, Catholics gave four hundred and ninety-one dollars, Protestants two hundred and ninety-four dollars. The question of merit ("deserve") has a much greater effect on Protestant giving than on Catholic giving!

Among the sixth of the population who say that they were not asked to contribute more, Catholic and Protestant contributions were about the same: three hundred and sixty-four dollars, higher than average for Catholics and lower than average for Protestants.

Not being asked and feeling that charities do not deserve the money, far from depressing Catholic giving to the Church, seem to increase it! Possibly, the explanation is that Catholics interpreted this question to apply to non-religious charities only. Those who either did not like such charities or were not approached by fund-raisers had more money available to give to their church. Protestants, on the other hand, might not have distinguished so sharply between "charity" and "church."

Whatever is to be made of this odd pattern of response, one cannot find in it any explicit evidence of anger towards the church or absence of fund-raising efforts by the church.

Might the Protestant fund-raising customs of requiring an annual pledge of a fixed proportion of income account for the greater financial contribution of Protestants?

In fact, there is no difference between the two denominational groups in the proportion that gives a fixed amount--"as in making a pledge"; approximately two fifths report such a practice. Protestants are significantly more likely, however, to give a percentage of their income to the church every year, thirty-two percent versus twenty-two percent.

Both the practices, however, correlate positively with high contributions. Catholics who give a fixed amount contribute five hundred and seven dollars, Protestants, eleven hundred and twenty-two dollars. Catholics who give a certain percent contribute seven hundred and eight dollars, as opposed to thirteen hundred and forty-four dollars for Protestants.

Finally, does religious devotion itself have any differential effect on giving for Protestants and Catholics?

Twenty-two percent of the Catholics and twenty-seven percent of the Protestants say that their religious beliefs affect their charitable contributions, a difference that is not significant and a response that, on the face of it, is highly improbable given the fact that religious contributions account for two thirds of all contributions in the country. Might it be, however, that the differences between Catholics and Protestants will be more acute among those for whom religious belief is perceived as a less important influence on charitable contributions?

Fifty-four percent of Catholics and fifty-nine percent of Protestants report that religion is a very important influence in their lives. While this difference, like the one described in the previous paragraph, is not statistically significant, might the largest differences among Catholics and Protestants be among those for whom religion is not important?

Figure 3.6
Annual Contribution
By Denomination and Importance of Religion

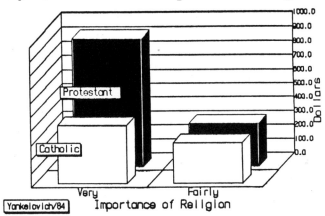

Figure 3.7
Annual Contribution
By Denomination and Church Attendance

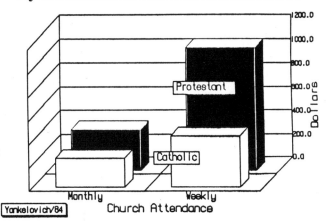

Some fifty-seven percent of Catholics and forty-five percent of Protestants report that they attend church almost every week, proportions which are compatible, given different wordings of questions and response patterns, with other studies of American church attendance. Might it be that the lower levels of Catholic contributions are to be found especially among those who go to church less often, especially since there was a sharp decline in Catholic Mass attendance in the years between 1968 and 1975?

In fact, the answer to all three questions posed in the preceding paragraphs is "No." The greatest differences between Protestants and Catholics are among those for whom religion is an important influence on their charity, among those who think religion is important in their lives, and among those who attend church every week (*Figures 3.6* and *3.7*).

Catholics who say that religion does not affect their contributions give three hundred and twenty-five dollars to their church; Protestants in the same category give five hundred and eighty-seven dollars. But among the minority who say that religion does affect their charitable giving, the contributions rise to five hundred and twenty dollars for Catholics and one thousand and eighty-eight dollars for Protestants.

Approximately half of each group (fifty-two percent of Catholics and fifty-six of Protestants) say that religion is very important in their lives; but this "importance" has very different financial implications. For Protestants, it means a contribution of nine hundred and ten dollars a year; for Catholics, it produces a contribution of four hundred and twelve dollars a year. On the other hand, among those who think that religion is only "fairly" important, the difference between Protestants and Catholics is only thirteen dollars--a three-hundred-and-two-dollar annual contribution for the former and a two-hundred-and-eighty-nine dollar donation for the latter. The difference between Protestants and Catholics in gifts to their churches is concentrated among the devout.

Finally, Protestants and Catholics who attend church a couple of times a month are separated in their contributions by only a hundred dollars. The former give three hundred and fifty-four dollars a year and the latter two hundred and fifty-one dollars a year. But the difference soars among those who go almost every week--four hundred and forty-six dollars for Catholics and one thousand and thirty-nine dollars for Protestants. The move from several times a month to weekly thus causes a Catholic to give approximately two hundred dollars a year more to his/her church, a Protestant to give almost seven hundred dollars a year more.

To look at it from a different perspective, the weekly church-going Protestant gives almost twenty dollars a Sunday, the weekly church-going Catholic contributes a little more than eight and a half dollars a Sunday. If one assumes that ten million families or unrelated individuals of Catholic orientation attend church every week, the difference between what they give and what they might give if they matched the Protestant generosity is eighty-five million dollars a week as opposed to two hundred million dollars a week.

We have not succeeded in accounting for the difference between Catholics and Protestants in annual donations to their churches. However, we have eliminated some of the reasons that have been adduced to explain these differences. Catholics are not poorer than Protestants nor up against the wall financially, either because of family size or costs of Catholic education. Nor could we find any evidence of lack of generosity in Catholic behavior and attitudes. On the contrary, Catholic social attitudes towards the poor, the less developed countries, and those beyond the community indicate greater social consciousness among Catholics.

Moreover, the differences are narrowest at the lower end of the socio-economic scale--among those who did not graduate from high school and those who earn less than fifteen thousand dollars a year and among those who report no "disposable" income (in the latter group Protestants in fact give less than Catholics).

The differences are also especially strong among the devout, whether devotion is measured by the importance of religion in their lives or church-going or the importance of religion in motivating charitable contributions. Strong religious commitment produces much more generosity among Protestants than it does among Catholics.

The differences are generally invariant, that is, they exist in almost all age, educational, demographic, and economic categories; and none of the available variables can account for differences between Protestant and Catholic generosity to religion.

Our analysis of the 1984 data, then, establishes the fact that Catholics have a dramatically different financial relationship with their church than do Protestants: they give only about half as much in terms of dollars and proportion of income. However, having rejected many of the conventional explanations, we have not been able to find one that does account for the striking differences. Is there a different Catholic subculture of religious contributions, one that the immigrants brought with them and which has persisted into the present era?

Does the "snap-shot" of the 1984 study portray for us a situation that has always existed in American Catholicism or does it depict a change from an earlier era when Catholics were more generous to their church?

1.4 / THE PAST

In the early nineteen sixties, Protestants gave 2.2% of their income to their churches (as reported in the two SRC studies used in this report). In the middle nineteen seventies, the Protestant contribution continued to be 2.2%. Thus, Protestant church giving has been constant over the last quarter century. Catholic church support in the early nineteen sixties (as reported in both the SRC and NORC studies) was the same as Protestant giving--2.2%. In the middle nineteen seventies, however, Catholic contributions slumped to 1.6% of income. Thus, the 1.1% reported in 1984 represents a drastic decline in Catholic contributions.

In 1974, Catholics gave approximately three quarters of what they gave in 1963 (as measured by proportion of income). In 1984, they gave half of what they contributed in 1963.

Should this decline continue for the next decade, the 1994 level of Catholic contributions would be 0.8% of income and in 2004, 0.6%.

As will be noted in the next chapter, the Catholic decline is, in effect, the result of Catholics' contributions not keeping pace with inflation and rise in real income, as Protestants' did. Hence, even as a projection of present trends into the future, the 0.6% estimate for twenty years from now assumes that inflation continues at the rate of the previous twenty years. But the 0.6% figure means, in 1984 dollars, a loss of perhaps nine billion dollars in potential income.

Thus, the "snapshot" presented in the last chapter does not represent "the way things always were" but, quite the contrary, "the way thing's didn't use to be." It is the result of a decline, indeed a catastrophic decline, in Catholics' generosity to their church. A quarter century ago, Catholics were as generous as Protestants. Now they are only half as generous (*Figure 4.1*).

(In line graphs, the black surface represents Catholics, the lined surface Protestants. The horizontal label indicates the year and the vertical the percent of income contributed.)

Figure 4.1
**Annual Contribution
By Denomination and Year**

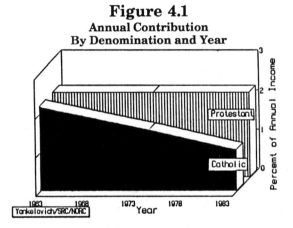

Figure 4.2
**Annual Contribution of Catholics
By Year and Church Attendance**

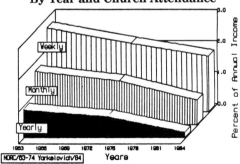

The decline is the sharpest among those who attend church every week. In 1963, they contributed 2.7% of their income to the Church. In 1974, their donation fell to 2.2% and in 1984, to 1.8%. Those who attended on a monthly basis declined from 1.7% to 1.4% to 0.8%; those who attended less than monthly gave at the three respective time points 0.9%, 0.7% and 0.5% (*Figure 4.2*).

Catholic church attendance declined sharply between 1968 and 1975. Thus, part of the decline in overall contributions must be the result of a larger proportion of the population in lower contribution categories; but within each category, contributions also fell. The smaller number of the devout gave smaller proportions of their income. The larger proportions of the less devout also gave smaller proportions of their income.

Even in 1963, devout Catholics gave less of their income to the Church than did devout Protestants. The steady rate of contribution by weekly church-attending Protestants over the last quarter century appears to be 3.5%, as opposed to a Catholic high for weekly attenders in the early sixties of 2.7%. Catholics achieved parity in average contribution because more of them went to church every week. Thus, part of the decline for Catholics can be attributed to lower levels of weekly devotion. However, even among the weekly attenders, the rate of giving fell from 2.7% to 1.8%, a decline of one third.

The decline is also sharp among the better educated: for those who went to college the rates were 2.4% in 1963, 1.9% in 1974, and 1.3% in 1984.

Those who did not graduate from high school fell from 2.0% to 1.6% to 1.3%. The group in between, the high school graduates who did not attend college, followed a path from 2.2% to 1.4% to 1.1% (*Figure 4.3*).

Figure 4.3
Annual Contribution of Catholics
By Year and Education

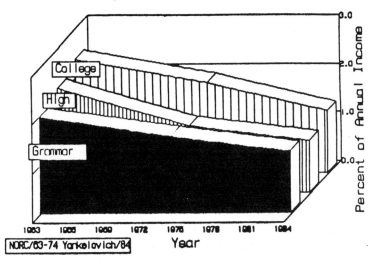

Figure 4.4
Contribution of Catholics by View
On Obligation to End Racial Segregation

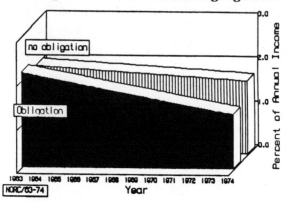

Figure 4.5
Contributions by Birth Control Attitude

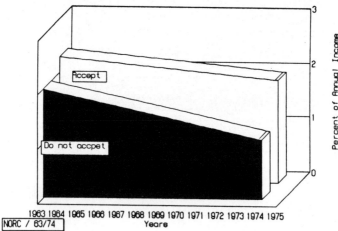

Figure 4.6

Rejection of Birth Control Teaching For Catholics by Year

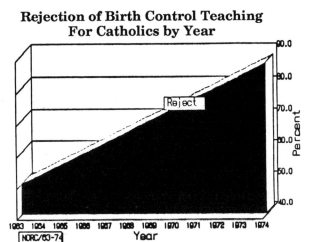

Figure 4.7

Contribution by Denomination and Belief Government Should Help Needy

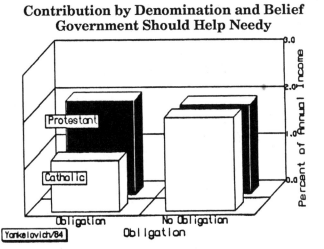

While the generosity of Catholics declined, then, in all educational and devotional groups, the decline was especially strong among those who had at least graduated from high school and among those who went to church with some regularity. The generosity of the less devout and the less well educated did not fall so sharply.

If the decline in financial contributions of Catholics can be taken as an indication of a certain sort of alienation from the institution, the question arises as to what "ideological" group is the most alienated. Much of the effort of church leadership during the years since the Council has been devoted to reassuring the more conservative Catholics--the ones who are the most likely to write letters of complaint to chancery offices. The image of devout but easily shocked laity who need reassurance that nothing essential or important is changing has had a powerful effect on the words and deeds of church leadership.

But in terms of financial contributions, are they the ones most likely to be alienated?

In 1963, those Catholics who thought that there was a personal obligation to work for the end of racial segregation gave 2.2% of their income to the Church. Those who thought there was no such obligation also gave 2.2% of their income. By 1974, the contributions of the former had fallen to 1.3% and of the latter to 1.7%. By this indicator, then, the "liberals" in the Church are more alienated than the conservatives (*Figure 4.4*).

Those who accepted the Church's teaching on birth control gave 2.3% of their income in 1963.

Those who did not (about half the Catholic population, even in 1963) contributed 2.0% to the Church. Eleven years later, the contributions of the former had fallen to 2.1% and the contributions of the latter (now representing seven eighths of the Catholic population) had declined to 1.5%. In our search in the next chapter for an explanation of the erosion of Catholic generosity, this striking difference must be kept in mind. At the present, it is enough to note that most of the decline seems to be among those who do not accept the official birth control teaching, a proportion that is now very high in the Catholic population (*Figures 4.5* and *4.6*).

Neither the birth control nor the race questions were asked in the 1984 study. However, questions about welfare, national and international, provide a rough standard of comparison to the race question.

Among those who think that the government has no obligation to guarantee food and shelter to help the needy, Catholics give 2.0% of their income to the church and Protestants give 1.9%. Among those who agree that there is such an obligation, Protestants give 2.0% of their income to the church and Catholics 1.1% (*Figure 4.7*). The more socially "liberal" Catholics, then, continued in 1984 as in 1974 to be more alienated from their institution, at least in terms of financial contributions, than the more socially "conservative."

As long ago then as the middle nineteen seventies, the decline in contributions among Catholics was in full swing. In *Catholic Schools in a Declining Church*, my colleagues and I estimated that the fall in contributions was causing the Church a per annum loss of 1.8 billion dollars. Catholics were, in fact, giving 3.8 billion dollars to the Church. If they had been giving at their 1963 rate (which we now know is the stable rate for Protestants for the last quarter century), they would have been giving 5.6 billion dollars. If the decline had stabilized in 1974, the annual loss in 1984 would have been half of the six billion current dollars that it presently seems to be.

The magnitude of the total loss over the last two decades is staggering, approximately sixty-five billion current dollars.

A tremendous number of schools, inner-city and suburban, could have been built and maintained with that money.

But are the schools themselves the cause of the declining contributions? In the last chapter, we saw that such an explanation does not seem probable. In this chapter, we are able to confirm that, at least in 1974, Catholic schools were not to blame for the decline in Catholic giving.

Those with children in Catholic schools were spending about three hundred and sixty-five dollars in tuition on these schools in 1974--on the average, 3.2% of their income. They were also contributing to the Church, in addition to their tuition, 2.1% of their income, substantially above the 1.5% contribution of those who did not have children in Catholic schools. Combining their contribution to the Church and their school tuition, the parents of Catholic school students were giving 5.3% of their income to parish and school. Indeed, their extra contribution and their tuition payments almost approached the cost of Catholic schools, which in that year was approximately eight hundred million dollars. If one added the higher contributions to the Church of those who had once attended Catholic schools, one could have made a case in 1974 that the Catholic schools not only supported themselves from higher Sunday contributions but indeed were a profitable enterprise for the Church.

In 1974, respondents were also asked whether they would contribute more money to keep the Catholic schools open and how much more money they would be willing to contribute. Four out of five said that they would. The aggregate income from their statements of how much they would give came to 1.7 billion dollars a year.

Even if they were exaggerating by half, the outcome of an appeal to help save the schools would have been almost nine hundred million dollars.

There is no way of testing the hypothesis, but one is permitted to wonder if one of the reasons for the decline of contributions to the Catholic Church is frustration over the failure of the Church to maintain its school system in the areas to which the Catholic population has moved in the last quarter century.

The Church leaders who thought that they could not afford to keep the schools open might have missed the fact that they could not afford to close them because by so doing they would lose the extra contributions of those who had attended such schools.

This analysis was originally presented in longer form in 1976 in *Catholic Schools in a Declining Church*. The conclusions that Catholic schools at least paid for themselves and that there were substantial additional resources (perhaps a billion dollars a year) to keep them open were so counterintuitive to Catholic educators and administrators that they were dismissed and forgotten. Hence, when told about the decline in Catholic contributions, the almost automatic response of clergy and religious is to blame the cost of Catholic schools.

I cannot understand this phenomenon. For some reason, more appropriately assigned to the research of abnormal psychologists than of sociologists, Catholic schools have become an inkblot for the clergy and the religious onto which can be projected many of their frustrations with the present condition of the Church and a scapegoat on which they can blame most of the current problems.

Against such attitudinal patterns, empirical research is a poor weapon. If you *know* that "our people can't afford the schools any more," then no evidence that they can afford them and are willing to pay for them is acceptable.

If you *know* that Catholic schools are an enormous financial drain on the Church, evidence that they virtually pay for themselves, that the parents of Catholic school children give more rather than less in the Sunday collections, and that the Catholic school graduates are more generous contributors is simply inadmissible.

Such attitudes present an impossible challenge to the empirical researcher: not only must he "prove" that his data are valid; he must also prove that certain convictions of his audience, unsupported by data, are wrong. Moreover, he must prove them to be wrong without the use of his own or any other empirical data.

Nonetheless, the data in the 1974 study show beyond any reasonable doubt that Catholic schools do not account either for the difference between Catholic and Protestant generosity or the decline in Catholic generosity during the previous decade (save perhaps that there maybe less Catholilc school alumni in the population). While there is no direct evidence of the innocence of the schools in the decline since then, the data presented in the last chapter about the "disposable" income of Catholics provides little support for the heart-rending clerical myth that "our people" are too strapped financially to afford the costs of Catholic schools and no evidence at all that tuition costs account for the decline in Catholic contributions. There would have had to have been a complete reversal in the behavior of Catholic school parents and an even more dramatic change of behavior than the one reported in this study to make the schools even a partial culprit for the erosion of Catholic generosity.

The portrait of lower Catholic generosity presented in the last chapter, then, describes not only an existing difference in generosity but a situation that results from a catastrophic decline in generosity of American Catholics over the last quarter century. In the early nineteen sixties, they gave as much to their church as a proportion of income as Protestants gave to their churches. In the middle nineteen eighties, they give only half as much. The loss in income amounts to some sixty-five billion current dollars. The decline seems to be especially strong among the more devout, the better educated, and the more "liberal" and cannot be blamed on Catholic schools or merely on the decline in regular Catholic church attendance.

In the next chapter, we will search for events peculiar to Catholicism during the last quarter century which may account for the catastrophe that we have described.

1.5 / EXPLANATIONS

The average American Catholic's contribution to the Church--as a proportion of income--has declined because Catholic contributions have not kept pace with inflation and with the rise in Catholic income.

Thus, American Catholics contributed an average of one hundred and sixty-four dollars to the Church in 1963 out of an annual income of $7,645. In 1984, their contributions had doubled to three hundred and twenty dollars but their income had almost quadrupled to $27,500. Much of this change in income was of course the result of the inflation of the late sixties and the seventies, although, on the average, real income (net of inflation) improved during the last two decades for Catholics as for other Americans *(Figure 5.1)*.

The inflation index in *Figure 5.1* is the Producer Price Index, which shows a 3.2 increase in the cost of living in the twenty-five-year period. That which cost a dollar in 1960 now costs three dollars and twenty cents. (The GNP Deflator, another measure of inflation, has also increased 3.2 since 1960.) Note that Protestant contributions in *Figure 5.1* not only have kept pace with inflation but have increased more rapidly with inflation while Catholic contributions have lagged behind the inflation rate.

The cost of living has approximately tripled between 1963 and 1984. To have kept pace with this change, Catholic income in 1984 would have had to rise to $22,935. Therefore, $4,565 dollars represents a "real," inflation-free improvement in "standard of living," a twenty percent increase in real income.

Catholic contributions have not kept pace with inflation. Protestant contributions have accelerated more rapidly than inflation and have kept pace with the increase in real income.

Catholics today, on the average, have more money available to give to the Church (and to Catholic schools) than they did in 1963. That is not, be it noted, a personal opinion; it is a statistical fact.

(When I mention this fact during the occasional lecture that I am still invited to give in Catholic schools, a priest will usually rise from the audience and say that it is not true in his parish. Perhaps it is not, but in a study of American Catholicism one is constrained to talk about national averages and not about particular parishes. Only if the vast majority of priests in this country claim that their parishes are different--and sometimes I have the impression that they do--would I suggest that they are not perceiving the situation accurately.)

Figure 5.1
Annual Contribution (Dollars)
By Denomination and Year

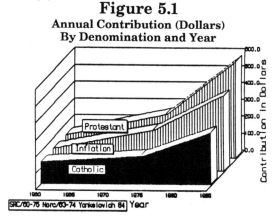

Many Catholic leaders will refer briskly to "inflation" as the cause of the decline in Catholic contributions (in inflation-free dollars and in proportion of income). But that leaves them, in the face of the data adduced in this report, with the question of why Protestant contributions kept pace with the changes caused by inflation and the increase in real income and Catholic contributions did not.

"Our people cannot afford to contribute more," one often hears it said, "because of inflation." In fact, they can afford to contribute more because their incomes have increased faster than inflation.

The image of the hard-pressed parishioner, struggling valiantly to keep up with rising prices while his/her income is not rising, tells more about the attitudes and needs of the priests and bishops who use it as an excuse than it does about the reality of the life of the average Catholic (which is not of course to deny that some Catholics are caught in such a bind, but merely to say that it is not typical).

Something must have happened in the Catholic community during the last quarter century which did not happen in the Protestant community.

The simplest explanation is that Protestants, since they are more deeply involved in the finances of their congregations, are more likely to be aware of the increased costs of administering a full-service local church than are Catholics and hence more realistic in making decisions about contributions. If Protestants have quadrupled their dollar contributions in the last quarter century, the reason, it could be argued, is that they are more aware than

Catholics that costs have quadrupled and that the apparently swollen parish budgets are not, in terms of any inflation-free dollars, any higher than they were in the early nineteen sixties.

There is no way to test this hypothesis with any of the existing data. Since most Protestants, however, are not likely to serve on budget committees and probably pay only the most minimal attention to congregational finances, the hypothesis can explain at the most only some of the failure of Catholic contributions to keep pace with the changing economic condition of the country.

It must be commented, however, that one rarely hears in funding appeals from Catholic clergy much reference with precise details to the effect of inflation on parish or diocesan budgets. Rather than being a specific multiplier, "inflation" seems in the Catholic financial approach to be a vague demon (like the southwest wind in Babylonian mythology) and indeed one not matched by the good angel of corresponding increase in dollar income (and some increase also in real income).

Therefore, not inflation as such but the inability of church leadership to respond to inflation may be a partial explanation for the decline in Catholic contributions. It is not likely, however, to account for more than some of the dramatic decline.

There are four other explanations which are offered, either singly or in combination:

1) The rise in educational attainment of Catholics and the resultant independence of the Catholic laity.

2) The changes created in Catholic life by the Second Vatican Council.

3) The decline in Catholic church attendance.

4) The effects of the birth control encyclical.

To test any of these hypotheses in a strict social science fashion, one needs measures of both contribution and the other variable at two points in time. One must show that the two variables are correlated at both points in time and that the change of one is linked to the change of the other. Two variables, correlations, simultaneous change--all three are therefore required.

(It is also possible that the strength of the correlation between the two variables increases between point one and point two.)

Thus, Catholic educational attainment has increased, education and financial contributions are correlated, and the two have changed in the last twenty-five years. But financial contributions correlated positively with educational attainment, so one would have expected an increase rather than a decline in Catholic financial contributions. The decline in contributions, then, runs against the trend of increased Catholic education. Moreover, the decline is equally distributed among all Catholic population groups as distinguished by educational attainments.

In 1963, the college educated gave 2.43% of their income to the Church; in 1974, they gave 1.92%; and in 1984, they gave 1.3%. The comparable rates of those who attended only grammar school are 1.97%, 1.58%, and 1.0%.

Thus, while Catholics act much more independently of Church leadership today than they did in years past, educational achievement does not seem to explain their failure to sustain previous levels of financial contributions.

Only one question was asked in 1963, before the end of the Vatican Council, about church reform--English in the liturgy. In 1963, seven eighths of the respondents supported English liturgy. In 1974, almost a decade after the end of the Council, the proportion was exactly the same. Hence, this reform of the Vatican Council, not having changed in the eleven-year period, cannot be the reason for the decline in contributions. There are no measures in the 1984 study on such matters of Catholic attitude and behavior, but it is unlikely that liturgical change, unconnected with the first half of the collapse of Catholic contributions, could be an important dynamic in the second half.

Moreover, in 1974, support for Vatican Council reforms correlated positively with financial contributions. Those who approved of the English liturgy and the other changes were likely to give more to the Church than those who did not. Since the majority of the Catholic population endorsed the changes (only about a fifth were opposed) the Council should have had, if anything, a positive instead of a negative effect on Church finances

Undoubtedly, the erosion of Mass attendance has had an effect on Catholic contributions, particularly since the Sunday-envelope form of contribution is tightly linked to Sunday (or Saturday afternoon) presence in church. But the decline in Mass attendance stopped in 1975 and the decline in financial contributions has not stopped. Furthermore, the most striking decline has been among those who go to Church every week--from 2.69% in 1963 to 2.15% in 1974 to 1.69% in 1984. On the other hand, among those who seldom go to church, the decline has been from 0.87% to 0.74% to 0.70% in 1984. If all Catholics went to Church every week and contributed as much as those who now go every week, their rate of contribution would still be only three quarters of that of Protestants.

Thus one is forced to consider the impact on Catholics' financial contributions of their changing attitudes on sex and authority. Both sets of variables are correlated, both declined from the early sixties to the middle seventies, and these declines were apparently correlated in the first decade of our research interest. Moreover, the correlation between birth control attitude and contributions increased during the decade.

There was no question about Catholic sexual attitudes in the 1984 study, but erosion of support for the traditional teaching has continued since 1974, as has decline in contributions.

Michael Hout and I have performed in "The Center Does Not Hold" (*American Sociological Review*, June 1987) a complex statistical analysis, using Rasch models, demonstrating that the changing sexual attitudes of Catholics have not affected church attendance since 1975 because of the intervention of a latent variable factor we call "loyalty." The intervention of this variable, which also inhibits Catholic political disaffiliation, is a mathematical and not a theoretical construct, much less, as has been suggested, a personal opinion.

Figure 5.2
Explanation of Decline of Catholic
Contributions Nineteen Sixty-three to Seventy-four

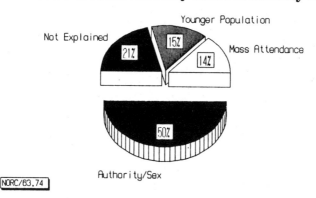

NORC/63,74

Figure 5.3
Catholic Contribution if Those Who Rejected
Birth Control Teaching Had Decreased at
Same Rate as Those Who Did Not

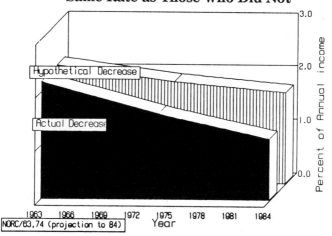

NORC/63,74 (projection to 84)

Analyzing the 1963 to 1974 change with a less complex mathematical model in *Catholic Schools in a Declining Church* (page 255), I concluded that fourteen percent of the decline could be attributed to the erosion of Mass attendance, fifteen percent to the influx into the population of a younger and less generous age group, twelve percent to changing attitudes on papal authority, and thirty-eight percent to a decline in acceptance of sexual ethics. A final twenty-one percent of the change was unaccounted for *(Figure 5.2)*.

Another way of explaining the phenomenon is to ask how much of the decline in contributions can be accounted for by the increase in the strength of the negative correlation between rejection of the Church's birth control teaching and financial contributions. What if the decline in giving among Catholics who reject the birth control teaching was no greater than the decline among those who accepted the teaching? What if, in other words, the correlation between the two was the same in 1974 as in 1963?

Figure 5.3 shows that the decrease, projected into the nineteen eighties, would have been less than half of what it actually has been. In other words, more than half of the decline in Catholic donations is associated with the increase in the proportion of Catholics who reject the birth control teaching and the increase in the negative correlation between rejection of the teaching and financial contribution. Not only did more Catholics reject the teaching, but their rejection had a greater effect on their contributions than did a similar rejection in

1963. The intervening event was the birth control encyclical.

Thus, of the various explanations for decline in Catholic contributions which have been offered, only the birth control encyclical explanation seems to fit the data, at least from 1963 to 1974. About half of the decline in Catholic contributions during that period can be accounted for by a parallel decline in the acceptance of Church teaching on authority and sex.

Partly because the models I was using in the middle nineteen seventies were, for the time, relatively complex, they were challenged in many Catholic circles--though mostly for their interpretation of the decline in Catholic religious behaviors other than those of financial contributions--on the grounds that they represented personal opinion or that they left out other forces at work in the Church.

In fact, then as now, the models are not personal opinions or value judgments. They are mathematical equations: the changes in sexual attitudes account mathematically for the changes in Catholic attitudes and behaviors, including half of the decline in financial contributions from 1963 to 1974. There are two pertinent issues and only two: whether the equations are properly calculated and which way the causality flows.

In principle, the causal flow could occur in four ways: the decline in contributions could be the result of the decline in acceptance of teaching on authority and sex; the decline in acceptance of teaching could be caused by the the decline in financial contributions; both could effect each other;

and both might be the result of some antecedent variable that causes them both to decrease and to which both are related, a variable we might call "alienation." The second and third explanations are improbable: declining contributions are not likely to change sexual attitudes. Therefore, either the first or the fourth explanation seems to be the proper one. Either changes in sexual attitudes, in direct defiance of Church teaching, have led to a decline of financial contributions or both are related to some prior influence. For the purposes of this report, which of these two explanations is chosen does not matter. If one chooses the "alienation" explanation, you must note that it is an explanation that nonetheless links contributions on the one hand with sex and authority on the other.

Note that this "alienation" has not affected either the reception of Holy Communion, which increased from 1963 to 1974, or the frequency of prayer, which increased from 1974 to 1984 (as measured in two other NORC surveys), or, since 1975, frequency of Mass attendance. It is an "alienation" from some teachings and from some institutional practices but not from church affiliation or ritual behavior, including in more recent years Mass attendance.

Last year, Hout and I reanalyzed the data from the two NORC surveys using different and more elaborate models and arrived at the same results. We then replicated the findings in other surveys from the early seventies to the middle eighties and arrived at the same conclusions: the decline in Catholic devotional behavior which began in the late sixties and ended in the middle seventies was associated with a rejection of the right of church authority to impose certain sexual standards on married men and women. My earlier findings, then, about the "alienation" related to attitudes on sex and authority seem to hold up.

Because of the absence of a question on Catholic sexual attitudes in the 1984 data, I cannot assert with complete confidence that the principle engine driving down Catholic contributions in the first half of the period under discussion is still at work in the second half of the period. Obviously, respect for official teaching continues to erode (now more on the subject of premarital sex than on birth control or divorce where almost nine tenths of the laity no longer accept the official teaching). Obviously, too, financial contributions continue to decline at the same rate as in the first half of the period. If the two decreases are no longer linked one to another, then another and unknown engine has intervened to continue the two erosions. Such a phenomenon is not impossible, but it is highly unlikely; it requires a new engine to account for half of the continuing decline in contributions.

It would appear that Catholics have elected a certain partial alienation from the institutional church, an alienation that can coexist with weekly Church attendance and other forms of ritual and community loyalty but which at the same time tunes out certain church teachings and contributes much less to the financial operation of the institution.

I will note here what I repeat at somewhat greater length in the next chapter: I am reporting the phenomenon of "partial alienation/partial loyalty" and not defending it.

For the scholarly sociologist of religion, this blend of alienation and loyalty is an extremely interesting and unexpected phenomenon, one that thus far seems to be limited to North America and the British Isles. The explanation of why it has occurred is beyond the scope of this report.

The point here is that the best explanation we have available from the empirical evidence for the slump in Catholic contributions is not to be found in inflation or greater education or the Vatican Council or a decline in Mass attendance or the costs of Catholic schools. The most useful explanation we have, accounting for half the slump, is a selective alienation related to a decline in acceptance of the Church's authority and especially its authority on sexual matters.

In the "picking and choosing" of this selective alienation, Catholics are choosing, perhaps semiconsciously, to give to the Church about half of what they gave in 1963 and about half of what their Protestant fellow Americans give today.

(An observation from Michael Hout: "A Dublin phenomenon: middle-class parishioners drop 20p in the basket just as the Christian Brothers taught them to do. They forget the fact that they now drive to the church in a Mercedes or Ford Grenada. When 20p was established as the normal contribution, the *Irish Independent* cost 5p. Now it costs 45p.")

My only mild dissent from the Bishop's comments in the second half of this book is that I am inclined to suspect from discussing these data with Catholic lay people that the anger at Church leaders which the data suggest is far more conscious than either he or I would have thought when we began our work.

It would be a mistake for those who lead the American Church to mislead and deceive themselves on the subject of lay anger.

1.6 / INTERPRETATIONS

In this chapter, I propose to step back from the data and from explanations tightly bound to the data and offer some interpretations and speculations about what they mean and what they imply for the future of fund-raising in the American Catholic Church. In the previous chapters, I relied on social science training and skills and not on personal instincts and opinion. In this chapter, I will present a more substantive and theoretical model to account for the catastrophic decline of Catholic contributions. This model is informed by the data and the analysis of the previous chapters, but the reader should be warned that it does not have the same scientific objectivity of those chapters. The reader must decide what merit to give to these interpretations.

I suggest that the phenomenon analyzed in the previous chapters can best be understood as the result of a failure of leadership and an alienation (here used in a broader sense than in the last chapter) of membership.

That the failure of leadership has been enormous I take to be obvious: the leaders of the Catholic Church, priests and especially bishops, have presided over a loss of income of monumental proportions without having responded to this loss in any effective fashion or even being aware of the loss, save in some of its effects.

Any other human organization in which a loss of half of its income, more than six billion dollars a year, had occurred would have engaged in intense soul-searching and policy reformulation. It would have also cleaned house of those who had permitted the decline and seemed unable to respond to it or even to recognize that it had occurred.

I realize that the Church is a unique organization, but I do not think that its special nature justifies complacency over a catastrophic decline in income.

Theologically, I would think such complacency might well be described as a sin of presumption.

Reforms will not have much effect unless there is an honest recognition on the part of church leaders of how badly they have failed and of the need not only to modify techniques but to substantially transform the attitudes with which they approach their laity in requesting funds. To proclaim that "now we are going to tithe" without understanding the implications of the relationship between financial contributions and alienation of the laity because of reasons of sex and authority is to whistle in the dark.

New techniques and methods announced blithely on Sunday morning from the altar or in the weekly edition of the diocesan paper or in a letter from the Chancery Office can confidently be expected not to work, no matter how wise or meritorious they might be. Any change must be accompanied by education, explanation, persuasion, and participation of the laity--arts which authoritarian church leadership has always found difficult.

I confess that I do not expect the fundamental attitudinal change that will be necessary if any innovation of techniques in fund-raising is to succeed. Men who would be wise enough to take the data reported in this study seriously and to transform their approach to funding would have been wise enough to have avoided the problem in the first place.

Short of any such change, I would not be surprised if the decline in Catholic contributions will continue in the next decade to something like 0.6% or 0.7% of income, unless the suspension of inflation of the last couple of years continues.

Leaders will therefore either tighten up budgets even more (which will mean a continuation of poverty wages to church employees, regardless of pastoral letters exercising a "preferential option for the poor") or insist on larger financial contributions in ways guaranteed to offend an already sullen laity.

It would be folly to demand tithing when the real problem is to persuade Catholics to double their contributions from one percent to two percent of their income so that they will catch up with their Protestant sisters and brothers. But to permit the contribution situation to deteriorate so badly in the first place is folly to begin with.

One cannot, it might be said, change church doctrines on authority and sexuality. In fact, changes now would be a waste of time because some nine tenths of American Catholics have made up their minds on these issues. But attitude and style can be changed.

If the laity are alienated and, as I read the data, sullen, the reason in substantial part is that they perceive the church leadership to be insensitive in its exercise of authority--and especially authority on the subject of marital sex. There is nothing more likely to offend married people than the apparent pontification of celibate bishops on the subject of what goes on in the marriage bed, especially when, as they see it, the pontification goes on in the name of Jesus, who seems to have had nothing to say on the subject.

If one listens to Catholic laity, one often hears nothing but complaints: terrible sermons; inept counselling; arbitrary rules and regulations, particularly at the time of reception of the sacraments; incompetent and arrogant financial administration; authoritarian leadership; insensitivity and cruelty to people with serious problems; little regard for the rights and dignity of women; pederasty in the clergy; dishonesty in the making and keeping of promises; two-faced stands on controversial issues; simplistic stands on politics and economics which display little awareness of the complexity of the issues involved; hypocrisy; amateurism; and disregard of how important sex is in healing and sustaining marriage.

Moreover, many lay people read in the press about the various scandals in the church: Clavi, Sidona, the Pauline Fathers, Reno, Chicago. They wonder how much of their money is going to sinister Italian organizations like the P-2 lodge or into the private homes of friends of bishops. Or how much of it disappears into the Vatican Bank. Or whether John Paul I was really murdered. Nothing the Vatican does by way of responding to such events tends to reassure the Sunday contributor.

And many also feel that every time the Pope opens his mouth it is either to put down women or to suppress freedom or to forbid married sex.

(I realize that this is an unfair and unnuanced interpretation of the Pope's position. It is, unfortunately, how he is perceived from the thirty-second clips on TV, the seven-hundred-word-press association reports from Rome, and the column or two in the weekly news magazines.)

Sometimes, I think that we priests and bishops have done everything we possibly could to drive away the laity during the last twenty years and that if we have failed it is not our fault. There is probably nothing much left which we can do now that will alienate them any more.

It is a savage indictment. "We are not like that at all," the leadership will say.

Perhaps not, but gentlepersons, that is how a very large proportion of your weekly church-attending laity perceive you and the reason they are unwilling to give you as much of their money as their Protestant counterparts are willing to give to their church leadership.

All right, how many feel that way?

To answer that question exactly would require another study, but on the basis of the data available and especially with the facts of the decline of financial contributions before us, I would guess that about four fifths of the laity have, at least to some degree, the attitudes described in the previous paragraphs and that perhaps half the Catholics in America picture church leadership pretty much the way I described it.

I exaggerate?

Then how come you're not getting that other six and a half billion dollars?

It is difficult for a church leader to admit that even among his most devout and dedicated people alienation exists, even as the word was defined in the last chapter. It cannot really be the case, can it, that four fifths of those who go to Mass every week reject the birth control teaching? And that contributions from these weekly churchgoers have fallen to fifty percent of what they were twenty years ago?

First of all, to admit such truths publicly would offend the Holy See, however true they may be. If you are a bishop, you do not tell the truth if it will offend Rome. Secondly, if you admit these facts to yourself, then it is hard to live with your public silence and equally hard to figure out what to do next.

So you deny them and do not listen to those who tell you about them.

What of the future? Hout and I have prepared projections based on life-cycle curves for the cohorts of Catholics born before 1965. On the basis of these projections, we see no reason to expect further decline in church attendance, at least for the rest of this century. And there is surely no reason to expect a turnaround among the faithful in their sexual practice issues, no matter how many catechisms are issued. Will the level of Catholic financial contributions improve? Only if · there is a change in basic attitude as well as techniques; and there is little reason to expect such a change at the present time.

In conclusion, I wish to anticipate the objections that are usually aimed at reports like the present one or, more precisely, at newspaper and TV accounts of them: The Catholic Church does not make ethical decisions by taking surveys. Good Catholics should do what the Pope says and should also support their pastor; if you reject the birth control teaching and don't contribute as much as you can to the Church, you're not a good Catholic, hardly a Catholic at all. Greeley is merely offering his personal opinions on birth control again. Or he is merely engaging in his old game of bishop bashing (revealing his authority fixations or his frustration because he is not a bishop).

These objections, having been delivered, usually satisfy the one who makes them and enable him/her to dismiss the findings as not worth further consideration. All the objections confuse fact with value, the report of an empirical situation with approval of it, the herald of bad news with the bad news he brings.

In fact, I agree that public opinion surveys are not the norm of ethical truth. I also agree with the Pope that they are one way but not the only way of learning the "sense of the faithful."

If one wishes to expel from the Church those who do not accept the birth control teaching, then you will dismiss four fifths of your weekly churchgoers and you will violate canon law that says a baptized person ceases to be Catholic only when he formally renounces his faith. As to what and who is a "good" Catholic, that is perhaps under God's jurisdiction and not ours.

Whatever my personal opinion on the birth control issue (and it is not greatly different from that which Archbishop John Quinn presented at the Synod on the Family, namely that more dialogue with the married laity is needed), my conclusions about the impact of the issue on religious practice are based on data and not on personal opinions.

Finally, the issue ought not to be whether I am bashing bishops, but whether what I say is true.

While the objections may satisfy the minds and hearts of those who make them, none of the objections will add one penny to the contributions made in Catholic churches in America next weekend nor solve by a single millionth of a percentage point the grim financial crisis that the leadership of the Catholic Church in this country seems to have created for itself.

1.7 / RECOMMENDATIONS

Policy recommendations from a sociologist are two steps removed from his data. Before he can recommend, he must first explain, as I did in the last chapter. Then, on the basis of his explanation, he must suggest changes that might constitute effective responses to the problems he has described in his analysis and the explanation he has provided for these problems. At each step away from the data, the sociologist must, if he is responsible, be more tentative.

On the other hand, no one else has a more solid basis for policy recommendations.

Policy makers ought to take seriously the recommendations of scholars who have studied their problems, but they also ought to realize that the construction, for example, of mathematical models does not quite invest the scholar with the fiery horns of Moses come down from Sinai.

With this caution I offer the following four policy recommendations:

1) The laity must be won back.

2) Those who give the money must have some share in deciding how it is spent.

3) Contributions should be be based on an annual, budget-based plan.

4) The rates of giving established by Protestants should be offered as guidelines for Catholic contributions.

5) A new theology of giving must be constructed, one that attends to the peculiar

conflicts about money which seem to exist between the clergy and the laity.

1) The Laity Must Be Won Back.

I begin with a parable.

In a certain very affluent parish with which I am familiar, a popular old pastor was retired a few years ago and replaced by a younger man who held a major position in the diocesan bureaucracy. By background and training, he was not qualified to deal with his well-educated, successful parishioners. He attempted to establish his importance the first Sunday by telling his people how little time he had for them because of his closeness to the bishop. Later, his office was phased out, but he continued to preach about its importance, even at First Communion Masses.

In a couple of months, he had antagonized many of the people in the parish by his personal and professional gaucherie; contributions declined; parishioners went to Mass at other parishes; the pastor began to preach about money every Sunday, making a bad situation worse; collections declined even more; the parish's half-million-dollar reserve at the Chancery Office dried up; and the pastor began secretly to prepare plans for a major remodeling of the church which would require a Chancery Office loan. Parishioners found out about this plan and organized a committee to oppose the reconstruction and loan.

The conflict was foolish and unnecessary, but the point here is that if one should approach such a parish with a plan for "tithing" or a demand for larger Sunday contributions or stern lectures about the obligation in "strict" justice to contribute to the support of the parish, one would merely aggravate an already terrible situation.

There are, alas, many such parishes in the United States.

Hence, church leadership should not even begin to think of new fund-raising schemes until it takes into account the disenchantment of the laity documented in this report and moves, humbly and sensitively, to overcome this disenchantment.

Obviously, the birth control teaching is not likely to be changed in the immediate future--and has indeed become irrelevant for most laity. Obviously, too, American church leadership is not able to prevent the Vatican from engaging in high-handed, authoritarian, and insensitive behavior.

However, it is not impossible to improve the quality of preaching, the skill of pastoral counselling, and the wisdom of administrative style. Pastors and bishops can learn to ask instead of ordering, to listen before talking, to consult before deciding, to consult instead of demanding. They can abandon the whole extra-canonical apparatus of regulations surrounding the reception of the sacraments. They can confess that the fund-raising efforts of the past have not been successful and ask the laity for help in joint efforts to resolve the Church's financial problems.

In the absence of a change in the style of pastoral leadership and in the quality of performance of pastoral tasks, any change in the tactics of fund-raising will be a waste of time, if not counter-productive.

It is not easy to be optimistic about the profound modification of episcopal and priestly behavior required in this recommendation. One changes only if one is prepared to be honest, even to oneself, about the mistakes of the past. Some priests are capable of such honesty and perhaps a few bishops. But it is much easier to follow the impulse to superficial pragmatism that is characteristic of the American Catholic Church: find a new gimmick, a fresh program, an untried technique, and use it without any question about how your people might respond or how you will determine whether it works or not.

To be blunt: if priests and bishops are not willing to change their manner of leading and administering, they should forget about trying to modify Catholic patterns of giving.

2) Those who give the money must have some share in deciding how it is spent.

This prescription may sound like a statement of simple justice, but it is not self-evident to the many Catholic clergy who feel that as soon as the money put in the collection box is locked up in the parish safe it becomes theirs to use as they see fit it.

The dictum is presented here, however, not as an ethical principle but as a statement of pragmatic realism: today's well-educated, independent American Catholic laity are no longer prepared to be silent partners in the administration of church funds. If you want them to give more money, you must permit them to share in the decisions about how the money is used--at parish, diocesan, national, and international levels.

Unless such participation is permitted, the lay people will feel that the money they have contributed is being put to uses of which they do not approve and that some/much of it is falling into the sinkholes of ecclesiastical scandals (*Banco Ambrosiano*, trials of pederast priests, friends of ecclesiastics, etc.). The fear is sometimes expressed that, if the laity had some participation in the control of church monies, they would veto social justice contributions. In fact, it is precisely those who are most likely to support such contributions who, as we have seen, are the ones most likely to be disenchanted with giving to the Church.

Moreover, one of the reasons that Protestant contributions have kept pace with inflation is that Protestant laity are familiar with congregational budgets and realize that ecclesiastical prices go up when all other prices go up. If one expects Americans to be responsible givers, one must give them some share of responsibility. In the absence of this responsibility, it is most unlikely that they will be responsible in their contributions.

This recommendation will not sit well with many priests and bishops. Financial control is the last bulwark of clerical power. To give it up would seem to mean the loss of the last prerogative of the once honored clerical caste. If you can't write the checks at your own discretion (whim), what is there left to being a priest or a bishop?

"I am Chicago," as one bishop is alleged to have remarked sometime ago.

Power is never given up easily, even when it is power that costs an organization six billion dollars a year.

It is not my purpose in this report to describe the structure and the mechanics of such lay participation in financial decision-making in the Church. There are many different ways such participation can be achieved. Whatever method is used, however, the participation must be *real*. The lay decision makers can be neither the creatures of the churchman, nor his rubber stamp. Any form of participation which leaves the churchman the same absolute power he has now (vis- -vis his people) will be quickly recognized for the sham that it is.

Is there not likely to be conflict between clergy and laity and among laity if such participatory procedures are instituted, especially while all sides learn the rhetoric and the techniques which can make such negotiating processes relatively smooth?

Our Protestant brothers and sisters seem to have routinized such joint decision-making so that it works reasonably well. Joint decision-making requires more time, of course, and more effort and more patience.

It also seems to produce more money.

3) Contributions should be based on an annual, budget-based plan.

In the autumn (or in the months before the parish's fiscal year begins), a parish budget should be prepared and distributed to the people with an indication that the budget divided by the number of families in the parish suggests a certain sum as the annual family contribution.

A $750,000 budget, for example, divided by fifteen hundred families requires an annual per family contribution of five hundred dollars (one hundred and eighty dollars more than the current national average--ten dollars a week instead of six).

Parishioners should then be asked to make a pledge of their annual contributions. The parish will mail monthly or quarterly reminders. The Sunday offerings then could be used for the poor, and the principle fund-raising of the parish would be taken care of by mail instead of by Sunday contribution.

Some parishes, I am told, are already experimenting with such schemes, even to the extent of asking parishioners to authorize their banks to make monthly contributions to the Church or accepting *VISA* and *Mastercard* payments!

Implicit in this proposal--about which (must I say it?) experiments should be made before it becomes universal policy--is the abandonment of the Sunday collection envelope as the principle means of fund-raising in American Catholicism. It was not, despite the reverence and awe which exist for it in many places, a system written on the stone tablets at Sinai, nor the eighth sacrament.

The collection envelope was introduced in the nineteen twenties as a replacement for the "pew money" approach to church finances. It was appropriate for an era of Immigration and Depression. It is, however, too casual, too hit-or-miss, too informal, too chancy, and (dare one say it) too "amateurish" for an educated population in an ecumenical age and an age when most middle-class folk organize their financial life around checkbooks and credit cards.

How many pastors are aware of the last-minute chaos on Sunday morning (or Saturday afternoon) when final preparations are being made for the trip to church and both the checkbook and the collection envelope box are not to be found?

A last minute dash is made for the church without either checkbook or envelope with confidence that there is an adequate amount of money in purse or wallet to make the appropriate weekly contribution. Then it is discovered that either or both are bare.

Well, we'll make it up next week.

If we remember.

I often wonder how much money is lost to the Church by such chaotic crises in family life.

Does any other voluntary organization in America use collection envelopes at its regular assemblies?

Such an approach would also mean the end of the "money sermon"--one of the most resented and despised (and frequently counterproductive) practices in American Catholicism. There are still some pastors, I fear, who find a periodic exercise in ranting to their people about money a means of reassuring themselves about their masculinity. I have never heard from a layperson who enjoyed such embarrassing episodes.

There are, in this age of the United States Postal Service, desk-top publishing, telephones, videotapes, and other means of communication, many less objectionable ways of talking about the parish's financial problems. Better that the Gospel be preached on Sunday (hopefully well preached) and the fund-raising left for finance meetings and visits (perhaps) by laity to the homes of their fellow parishioners to explain the parish financial situation.

You don't like another layman coming to your home to discuss your contributions with you?

Tell that to your Jewish brothers and sisters.

Is there some risk in such a drastic change of approach to parish financing? Not if the change takes place cautiously and after consultation with and explanation to and participation of the members of the parish. To assume that what little generosity the laity still have will vanish because the collection basket is not shoved in front of them on Sunday is to do them a great injustice.

When my first pastor decided in 1955 to abandon pew rent and ask the people to make up for it by putting an extra quarter in their collection envelopes on Sunday (most of them college-educated professionals), he went through the torments of the almost damned for fear the single collection would somehow not be quite as large as the combination of the two.

In fact, the single collection was substantially higher than the combination of the two.

The poor man said grimly that he was afraid that it would not last.

Need I say that it did last?

But I have wondered what kind of model of the attitudes of his people lurked in his skull. He seemed to imagine them as cunning, stingy folk looking for some way to cheat the Church out of its due and ready to jump on any excuse for curtailing their contribution.

He used to falsify his annual fiscal report, too, for fear if the people knew how well the parish was doing, they would diminish their collections.

Such strange models of lay behavior still exist in the minds of many church leaders, where they have become self-fulfilling prophecies. If you don't trust your people, then their behavior is likely to be untrustworthy. Catholic contributions, one must say it over and over again, are low not because of the lack of the spirit of generosity among the Catholic people but because of their resentment about the way the Church behaves towards them, because of their lack of participation in the fiscal process, and because they do not understand the costs of running a modern, full-service parish (the third reason in great part because of the second).

If penury is the problem, then no reform will work. But there are no reasons to think the Catholic laity are miserly. Rather, they are uninformed, ignored, and angry (the last in substantial part because of the first two).

Hence, the program envisaged in this recommendation is not as reckless as it might seem to a priest or a bishop who does not trust the fundamental generosity of his people.

4) The rates of giving established by Protestants should be offered as guidelines for Catholic contributions.

Consider *Figure 7.1* which presents data about the contributions in 1984 of Protestants and Catholics who attend church every week. The level of income has very little effect on Catholic contributions. Those who earn under twenty thousand dollars contribute 1.2% of their income to the Church; those who earn between twenty and forty thousand contribute 1.3% of their income to the Church. And those who earn more than forty thousand dollars a year contribute 1.0% of their income to the Church.

Their Protestant counterparts contribute, respectively, 2.7%, 3.3%, and 4.2%.

Figure 7.1
Contributions to Church by Income and Denomination (Weekly Attenders)

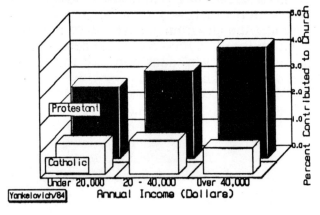

Thus, it is entirely fair to tell the regular churchgoers who earn, let us say, fifty thousand dollars a year, that, on the average, they should be giving a little more than two thousand dollars to the Church--about forty dollars a week.

Most affluent Catholics, making their contributions in the Immigration and Depression method of the Sunday collection and with pre-inflation notions about parish costs, would scream bloody murder.

They cannot possibly afford such generosity.

To which the obvious reply is that their Protestant counterparts can afford it, but of course we are not telling you what you must do, we are merely offering the norm of your Protestant neighbors as a guide to your conscience!

And those who are earning thirty thousand dollars might be told that an appropriate contribution for them would be approximately a thousand dollars a year.

They'll scream just as loudly.

Note that in *Figure 7.1* the appropriate demands for the weekly attenders who earn less than twenty thousand is a doubling of their contribution, for those who earn between twenty and forty thousand a little less than a tripling of their contribution, and for those who earn more than forty thousand dollars a quadrupling of their gifts.

Such is the measure of the failure of all of us Catholics who, for whatever reasons, have not sustained a level of giving comparable to that of our separated brothers and sisters.

Obviously, the use of these data to establish guidelines would only be prudent--in my judgment--when the other four recommendations have also been followed.

5) A new theology of giving must be constructed, one that attends to the peculiar conflict about money that seems to exist between the clergy and the laity.

Catholic giving practices are not underpinned at all by any clearly thought out theological rationale. The former rationale--you give the money to us because we ask for it and because you are loyal--no longer has much appeal. Priests are astonishingly insensitive to the dissatisfactions of the laity with current fund-raising practices and attitudes. Laity are deeply, sometimes irrationally, angry at the fact that priests get paid for incompetent performances and then assume that they can do whatever they want with the funds that they (the laity) contribute. Giving has become an inkblot onto which all the frustrations of both sides can be projected. A new theology that will clear away the mutual frustrations is essential. The bishop moves in that direction in his afterword. It will be interesting to see if Catholic theologians will take time off from their preoccupation with offering political advice to the world to reflect on the story reported in this book.

What are the chances of these five modest recommendations being accepted? Probably less than that of the College of Cardinals converting *en masse* to Mormonism.

The financial condition of American Catholicism will, I fear, get worse--much worse--before it gets better.

A BISHOP'S AFTERWORD

William McManus

2.1 / SOME PERSONAL

REFLECTIONS

I enjoy a cherished distinction: I am one of a few United States bishops whom Father Greeley has not, to use his word, "bashed" for incompetence, ineptitude, and spinelessness. In one of his Catholic press columns (12/18/76)--now, a little like him, rather aged--he declared that I am "one of the great bishops of the country" and that my appointment to be Ordinary of the Fort Wayne-South Bend, Indiana, diocese was "one of the best in the hierarchy in the last fifteen years." In his autobiography, *Confessions of a Parish Priest*, I receive a couple of pleasant commendations, including his gratitude for my being "loyal."

The truth is he should have "bashed" me.

Father Greeley and his professional colleagues culled out of voluminous social science research abundant evidence to support continued expenditures for most existing Catholic schools and for the building of new ones in suburban areas to which thousands of Catholics had migrated. Despite all this data, I, in my position as a school leader in the Archdiocese of Chicago, was much more influenced by the insidious proposition that, however ideal they were and could be, Catholic schools in the nineteen seventies, unlike Catholic schools in the sixties, were out of the Church's financial reach and alternative methods of Catholic education should be initiated.

During the years of Vatican II and into the seventies, I watched the expansion of the Chicago Archdiocese's elementary and secondary schools come to an abrupt halt. In one of my first interviews with then Archbishop Cody in 1965, I unfolded some pending plans for new schools in new parishes and for additional high schools. He bluntly told me, "No more schools for awhile; they're too expensive. Put everything on hold."

I do not think he did this on his own initiative. In New Orleans, his episcopal appointment before Chicago, he had directed a vast amount of school construction, financed largely by bank loans. Rumors that he was financially irresponsible accompanied him to Chicago. In the archdiocese, some people in the inneɪ circle advised him to "stop McManus." "He's 'crazy' about schools," Archbishop Cody was told, "and always is thinking of ways to spend money for school buildings and teachers' salaries, money which the archdiocese doesn't have and won't be able to raise."

Like many other people in the Church or on the edges of it during Vatican II, Cardinal Cody was caught up in the prevalent emancipation mood, i.e., "get out from under if you can." A number of priests and sisters, unbearably restricted, they felt, by archaic rules and customs, left active ministry; many rank and file Catholics did not bother with their lapsed subscriptions to Catholic newspapers and periodicals; strident Catholic voices screamed for reforms, not the renewal envisioned by the Council; and discontent swirled around the notion that everything was up for grabs. Some bishops and pastors had the idea that Vatican II signaled the time "to get out from under" the financial burden of parish schools and other expensive activities. "Pay off the debt and don't bother the people about money" became the conventional post-Vatican II wisdom.

To Cardinal Cody's credit (some severe critics would say "discredit"), he launched what appeared to be a last-ditch effort at raising a large sum of new money for a variety of purposes, including subsidies for inner-city Catholic schools and, in a sort of a wild dream, for brand new, highly innovative total learning centers for adults and children in black neighborhoods. Called "Project Renewal," capitalizing, as it were, on the renewal proposals of Vatican II, it got caught in a mess of controversies, largely unrelated to its appeal for increased donations in the form of pledges. There was controversy about whether the Church really was rich or poor and about who would say how the money was spent. There was also bitter resentment directed against the professionals who threatened to tell the Cardinal if a parish did not cooperate.

A near mortal blow was struck against Project Renewal when Cardinal Cody, largely at my insistence, jumped into the middle of a tumultuous dispute about busing for racial integration. Thousands of parishioners canceled their pledges to Project Renewal after they heard the Cardinal's letter, read at Sunday Mass, asking Catholics' moral support for the Chicago public schools' busing program and announcing that Catholic schools would have a busing program of their own to promote racial integration in mainly all-white, suburban Catholic schools. Some critics in the "he can do nothing right" school alleged that the Cardinal merely hopped on the liberal bandwagon for racial integration in schools and that he really did not believe in it anymore than he did in the schools themselves. I disagree. Regardless, Project Renewal's faults dulled interest in archdiocesan-wide fund-raising. The interest still is dull.

Though what I have said is local to Chicago, similar sad sagas could be recited about other arch-dioceses and dioceses during the post-Vatican II era. The dominant mood seemed to be: "Things in the Church are too upset to settle into a serious drive for more money; let's do the best we can with what we have."

It was not that way before Vatican II. In the late nineteen fifties and sixties, when I was superintendent of the Chicago Archdiocese's Catholic schools (the nation's largest Catholic school system, fourth largest of all U.S. systems), the situation was much different. Again, I will write about Chicago because I know it well and it is, I think, an illustration of what happened elsewhere.

In the sixties, simple rules, perhaps better called practices or procedures, prevailed.

1. Build what needs to be built and be confident that the people will pay for it.

2. Borrow from banks whatever funds are necessary to begin and to complete the project and be trustful that the people will pay off the loans in ten, twenty, or thirty years.

3. Build the school before the church. Usually, that meant constructing a sixteen- or twenty-four-room school building with part of it set aside for a temporary church. In a short time, an influx of children would crowd out the church, thus

necessitating construction of a church building.

4. Move with the people; do not turn pupils away from our schools; and take risks.

Those were days more hearty than heady. Church leadership, not especially brilliant or well organized, was swept along by post-war economic prosperity, an unprecedented baby boom, and the widespread conviction that the Church, though a little stuffy and archaic, had grand, lovable traditions worth a considerable amount of personal sacrifice. Busy with buildings, the church leadership, including myself, gave scant attention to the enterprise's human dimension--e.g., the pitiably low stipends paid to nuns (who now are rightfully calling for Seventh Commandment restitution) and the miserable wages paid lay employees. Moreover, there was no planning in accord with professional standards, no in-depth demographic studies (it was simply presumed that the baby boom would go on forever), and no careful analysis of church finance in light of the nation's short-term and long-term economic condition. In the sixties, there was little alarm over clear signs of the beginning of the end of religious vocations. Plunge in, push ahead, hope for the best--this was the hearty, maybe a bit unreasonable, motivation for the Church's somewhat reckless spending, centered much around the schools, during the felicitous sixties. And the money rolled in, at least enough to pay current expenses and interest on debt. Three or four percent interest on a debt was no great worry.

I can daydream for hours about those up-beat years in the sixties and enjoy every moment. The only nightmare is that the sixties gave way to quite different seventies. Returning to my remark about Father Greeley's failure to "bash" me, I have to admit that I had more power--if I may use that word--during the seventies than I had in the sixties. I was a bishop (sort of one as a Chicago auxiliary), the secretary of Catholic education (a position which I blew because of my total lack of under-standing of the group dynamics necessary for deci-sion-making in the seventies), and a two-term, three-years-each, elected chairman of the education committee of the bishops conference. In this last position, I unwisely gave a lion's share of attention to the cause of legislation to fund Catholic schools with government money. My reasoning (it was somewhat naive, I now think) was that a crusade for government aid to Catholic schools, even if it were unsuccessful, would generate enthusiasm and pro-duce private support of them in lieu of the govern-ment funds denied them. But the opposite hap-pened. When Catholics were denied a fair share of tax money for their schools, they felt like giving up on them altogether. No doubt about it, repeated de-feats of nonpublic school aid proposals in legisla-tures and courts discouraged the Church from starting new schools and from launching fund drives to maintain the high quality of those already in business. I do feel, however, that I was faithful to the guideline in Pope Pius XI's *Encyclical on Christian Education*, which said: "Catholics will never feel, whatever may have been the sacrifices already made, that they have done enough for the support and defense of their schools and *for securing laws which will do them justice.*" (Italics added.)

What happened in the nineteen seventies? Only a handful of new schools were started. Hundreds closed down. Some inner-city Catholic schools either quit or barely survived. Everywhere, the alleged explanations were "no money; too costly; can't afford lay teachers; Catholic schools have seen their day; the only solution is government aid, and that's not coming." It seems to me, and Father Greeley is sure of it, that at the very time the Church urgently needed its schools to educate the young for active, fruitful membership in the post Vatican II Church, it let many of them fade from the scene--diminished, distraught, and woefully threatened by financial difficulties.

In Chicago, I only whimpered (I should have screamed) when newly appointed suburban pastors decided to build community centers with makeshift religious education (CCD) classrooms in preference to starting a school that would be followed by a church. Much to the distress of Cardinal Cody, I did yell about cutbacks of subsidy to inner-city schools, even going so far as to propose that every casket buried in Chicago's Catholic cemeteries (twenty thousand caskets a year) should be sealed with a fifty-dollar decal reading "for inner-city Catholic education." That would have produced a cool one million dollars!

Chicago, however, did institute a "twinning" project whereby affluent parishes *on their own initiative* assisted inner-city parishes, mainly those with schools. "Poor" pastors did not have to go begging; well-healed parishes sent their pastors out to find other parishes in need of help. Cardinal Cody extended the program so that every parish in the archdiocese, however meager its resources, helped another parish. For a parting shot at Chicago, I would like to say that if every suburban parish without a school would donate to inner-city schools an amount equal to what its subsidy for its own parochial school would be, then much of the financial plight of Chicago's Catholic inner-city education would come to an end.

In 1976, I was moved from Chicago to Fort Wayne-South Bend, Indiana. Because of my record, the natives feared that their new bishop would be a "school nut," so preoccupied with Catholic schools that he would give scant attention to anything else. Their fears were groundless. My own boss at last, I tried to see the whole, big picture of the many needs and opportunities in the diocese. It did not take long for me to realize that, first of all, the diocese was overbuilt but understaffed--with many under-utilized structures and not enough employees. In addition, those on staff were poorly paid. My motto became "People before buildings," and of course, I ran head on into financial problems. I sweated them out. For the first six years, 1976-1982, it took the best in me to raise the diocese's total income in all places from all sources at a rate equal to inflation. It was a "no progress" undertaking--no new ventures of any size, no new schools, and no substantial improvements in salaries. The last three years, we (great priests, religious, laity, and I) managed, finally, to give employees real increases, not mere upward adjustments to match inflation.

Raising more and more money every year entailed a great deal of pastoral pain--meeting frequently with advisors; conferring with pastors; answering criticisms; searching for an equitable formula to tax parish funds for diocesan projects; and worrying about investments and interest rates. Though I was blessed to have had an extraordinarily talented and efficient business manager who relieved me of much attention to management details, I had to make the tough final decisions on basic policies.

Now that I am retired and have a little time to reflect on the past and to speculate about the future, I have a renewed interest in whether Roman Catholics in the United States can afford the donations needed to finance the Church's ever more costly enterprises and services--not only its schools but the multitude of new activities related to a well-planned, post-Vatican II ministry.

2.2 / IS THERE ENOUGH MONEY?

One economist who knows what he is talking about directly answered a question I put to him in 1973. His name is Father Ernest Bartell, C.S.C., an economist on the faculty of the University of Notre Dame. My question, voiced while I was a member of President Nixon's Commission on School Finance (meeting in the Watergate Hotel!), was: "Can Catholics afford to support Catholic schools in the foreseeable future?" His answer: "Envision all the money Catholics earn in one year from salaries and investments and see it in a huge pile. Of course, Catholics can afford to support the schools! The question is what size slice of the pie Catholics will put into the schools. And that is a question for educators, not for an economist."

I feel certain that any economist would reply affirmatively if asked whether all adult Roman Catholics in the U.S. have enough money both to support an updated, Vatican II form of church ministry and to include in this support just salaries for all employees. Whether these Catholics will donate sufficient money is a question not for an economist but for an ecclesiologist and a social scientist.

There is another way to put it. Father Greeley's data, as I read it, reveal:

1. Catholics in 1984 contributed *less* to the Church than did Catholics in 1964, i.e., as it is measured by dollars adjusted for inflation.

2. Church-going Catholics in 1984 gave less than did church-going Catholics in 1964.

3. From 1964 to 1984, Catholics moved up--
not down--the economic ladder. They
have much more gross and disposable income.

4. Catholics in general and Catholic churchgoers in particular now are giving much
less than their Protestant counterparts.

Obviously, Father Greeley's data are general
figures. Particular amounts of money which
Catholics have and how much of it they give to the
Church vary widely from diocese to diocese and
from parish to parish. These substantial variations
(about which I do not have specific data) immediately suggest the importance of much more cross-
funding--help from the affluent to the poor. The
U.S. bishops conference, its department for home
missions; the Catholic Church Extension Society,
headquartered in Chicago; and through several
other agencies, provide assistance to dioceses,
parishes, and institutions with proven need for financial assistance from outside sources. Most dioceses also have programs to help parishes whose
members cannot afford to contribute sufficient
funds to cover all expenses. The total of all these
programs is an expression of good will and generosity, but it is far from being a master plan to al-
locate equitably all the money which Catholics can
afford to give to their church. Far too often,
Catholics' donations are proportioned to what their
local parish needs rather than to what their incomes
would warrant for generous donations to the
Church. I have heard pastors say: "My parish is
completely built, out of debt, has no school, and

needs nothing more; so I never mention money to my parishioners. What they give is plenty for the needs of this parish." Parishes like that may be the ones whose parishioners' total contributions are less than one percent of their total gross incomes. I point no finger of blame. This phenomenon is perhaps a by-product of a great strength in the U.S. Church--its parochial pattern. But this pattern has a tendency to become selfish, myopic parochialism. It is a trend that should be checked and reversed.

2.3 / IS THE CHURCH THE PROBLEM?

For the balance of this afterword, I will offer some suggestions to reverse the downward trend of Catholic Church income and, hopefully, to start it on an upward path. These suggestions will allude to the commanding role that the U.S. Church's ecclesiology will play in its finances. The way Catholics see their church will substantially impact their financial support.

Catholics perceive their church as both a divine institution and a human organization.

They believe that Incarnate God, Jesus Christ, founded the Church to continue His total ministry to God's people--to redeem and save them from sin's dreadful consequences and to be, as He promised, the way, truth, and life for all Christians. Catholics also know that their institutional church is a human organization and, from day one, has had in its leaders and members an assortment of human beings, some heroically virtuous, others notoriously vicious, and most a mixture of sinfulness and holiness.

When typical Catholics have to make a decision on an amount of money to contribute to their church, they tend to think of it as a human organization, as another deserving claimant on their generosity. Many Catholics, I suspect, would think it more arrogant than pious to consider their donations for the parish church's light bills, air conditioning, heat, or maintenance of grounds as "gifts to God," whatever may be the religious motivations for their contributions. Sad to say, I fear that Catholics rarely see much of a connection between their donations and their worship. I will comment later on this sorry situation.

Almsgiving is something else. Most Catholics have a profound and hearty faith that a donation to feed starving people in Ethiopia or to send medical supplies to persons devastated by an earthquake or to arrange Christmas baskets for poor families is a response to Jesus' teaching that whatever they do for their sisters and brothers in need they do for Him. The almsgiving pattern among Catholics usually is spontaneous, generous, and transitory; and at least for its moment, it is primarily a religious experience, not, as some cynics say, a relief of guilt.

Catholics' perceptions of their church's human leadership correlate with their donations. These perceptions vary: some may see the bishop or pastor as an inspired leader with vision and courage; others may see the same person as an ambitious despot, feathering his own nest, cowardly, basically inept, and indecisive. (There are few adjectives, either complimentary or derogatory, which have not been appended to a bishop's name.) Far more important, however, as Father Greeley has emphasized, is the laity's general perception whether the Church's leadership is faithful to Jesus' gospel standards and ideals or whether this leadership, like that of the lawyers denounced by Jesus Himself, is "laying impossible burdens on people but will not lift a finger to lighten them."

Professional fund-raisers whom I interviewed told me that a bishop's or a pastor's popularity is a sure-fire factor in the success of a fundraising campaign. If the bishop or pastor has a high rating for leadership (even though some may disagree with his leadership, they know it exists and is sincere), then his constituents will give him a vote of confidence by increasing contributions to the diocese or to the parish or to both. Popularity, fund-raisers told me, centers on the religious, spiritual, charitable, and educational services that the diocese or parish has provided. Popularity, they said, does not require (and sometimes may be diminished by) a cleric's self-conscious, handshaking, back-slapping style. Integrity is a requisite component of genuine popularity.

Development directors in several dioceses who responded to an inquiry of mine about their recently successful fund-raising ventures all said that the local bishop's credibility--his openness to suggestions, follow-through on commitments, and high visibility in the diocese--is essential to enlist pastors' and parishioners' cooperation with a diocesan fund drive.

In my mind, there is little doubt that change and turbulence in the post-Vatican II Church, humanly viewed, have upset many Catholics, maybe all Catholics, in one way or another. This upsetting, however, has not been all bad, as some severe critics of Vatican II have asserted. On the whole, Vatican II was what Pope John XXIII intended: a refreshing appraisal of everything old to make its pristine beauty attractive and appealing in the contemporary world.

Some Catholics, however, became upset by what they thought (erroneously, I believe) was modernization (newness for the sake of newness) or renewal in the form of fads. Others were disturbed by the anti-authoritarian vocabulary of some Vatican II reformers. "Throwing everything up for grabs" (which is not at all what Vatican II did) caused much distress for those Catholics who long had believed their church was a safe haven and protection for their most cherished values and ideals.

There are, however, other Catholics, once impressed favorably by Vatican II's rhetoric, who now doubt whether any real changes for the better are firmly in place some twenty years after the Council's closing session. They do not feel good about their church's banging away at sexual immorality in a fashion that seems insensitive to the laity's experience of the place of sex in marriage and in human life itself. Others insist that church leadership still is trying to hem in the laity instead of opening up new opportunities for innovative lay leadership. The worst criticism I hear from the younger generation is that "the Church is a bore." I see nothing to be gained by telling them that their religious dullness sometimes is one reason the Church may bore them.

Many calm, reflective Catholics are inclined to say, ever so gently: "I don't know what's missing, both in the Church and in me, but the Catholic Church I love isn't grabbing me the way it should." And that may be the fundamental reason why Catholics are not grabbing at money in their wallets and purses to increase their donations.

In the first part of this book, Father Greeley delves into a number of possible reasons for a twenty-year decline in Catholic Church income. In this afterword, it would be foolish and futile for me to question his data . That would require a social science researcher's skill and experience, neither of which I possess in even their most rudimentary elements. Moreover, I make no pretense at an ability to interpret or to reinterpret his data. Data are facts, and that is about as close as mortal humans can get to truth.

From his professional analysis of the data available to him, Father Greeley has concluded that--in the absence of other documented reasons for the decline in the Church's income--two factors that may or do explain it are: (1) the Church's unyielding official position on contraception and (2) the caliber of a number of men now holding episcopal positions.

By way of comment, I doubt that a modification of the Church's official ethic on contraception would release a torrent of new money into the church treasuries. Furthermore, I doubt whether many Catholics *consciously* are holding back or holding down their contributions because of their disagreement with the Church's stand on contraception. *Subconsciously,* however, many Catholics, even some who are obedient to the position on contraception, may feel badly let down by the Church's failure to look more closely at the contraception issue in light of frightening social problems like over-population in some areas of the world, parental abuse of unwanted children, teenage pregnancies, etc. Subconsciously, too, married Catholics may feel that their church will not listen to them when they try to express their ideas about responsible parenthood in the real, hard world they know so well and about the prominent role sexual compatibility must have in a happy marriage. Official insensitivity, more than an adamant moral stance, may be discouraging generous contributions.

My amateur research, consisting of inquiries to fund-raisers and development directors, turned up a universal negative response to my question about whether the Church's position on contraception was cited by Catholics who refused to contribute to requests for funds. My results do not prove much. It is much easier for a non contributor to say, "I can't afford it," than to say, "I don't buy the Church's stand on birth control."

Father Greeley minces no words in his indictment of the U.S. bishops for their twenty-year failure to raise contributions at least at the same rate as inflation. That failure, he says correctly, has cost the Church billions of dollars which it might have had for the asking. With this money in hand, the Church could have moved ahead with its traditional construction and maintenance of schools and could have taken many steps toward reasonable salaries for church employees. Part of this episcopal failure is due, he says, to many bishops' shallow concept of leadership, i.e., "I have to do it all myself." If more bishops had sought and followed the counsel of lay persons expert in finance, then they would have been better managers. Freezing out the laity at both diocesan and parish levels may be what caused the long chill on church income.

Because I do not know enough about what happened in diocesan offices across the United States for the past twenty years, I am in no position to confirm or to deny Father Greeley's indictment. I will remark, however, that, during these years, many bishops were advised by lay leaders who often knew little about the Church and much about business. They advised that the Church should get out of debt, particularly because of the wildly inflated interest rates during most of that period. This preoccupation with getting out of debt put a damper on most proposals for diocesan expansion of ministries and buildings. By hindsight, I would say that the bishops should have paid more attention to ecclesiologists and sociologists who might have advised them about where the institutional church was headed and about the means needed to get to its correct destination.

Though Father Greeley's data unquestionably document the Church's two-decade failure to pace its income-producing efforts with inflation and with its need for new and additional ministry, there are other data which at least show that the Church's present financial condition might be much worse if it had not been for the vast amount of energetic fund-raising ventures undertaken between 1966 and 1986. During this period, at least ninety percent of the diocesan, parochial, and institutional fund-raising campaigns reported by organizations that keep records of these things have been a success. In many cases, the total amount pledged and collected has exceeded goals. Easiest by far have been appeals for new buildings--e.g., a new parish church, a renovated cathedral, a community center, or a new parish gymnasium (a sure bet); but annual appeals for maintenance and slight improvement of ordinary pastoral services--e.g., Catholic Charities--usually have been more difficult. In my research, admittedly incomplete, I did not come across a report of any diocesan or parish fund-raising program designed primarily and explicitly to increase church employees' salaries to a reasonable standard of a just wage. A few individual Catholic high schools and institutions of higher education have had successful appeals of this kind.

For several years, the National Catholic Stewardship Council has published an annual survey of diocesan fund-raising. The latest survey (1986) has a substantial amount of uncorrelated information too diffuse for me to put together into anything resembling a trend. I did notice, however, that more money was raised in 1985 than in 1984 in all the dioceses included in the survey (some large enterprises, like Chicago, are not included, presumably because they did not choose to make a report). Nevertheless, in almost half the dioceses, the amount was less than or barely equal to a very low inflation rate. Some dioceses, however, had large percentage increases, but I do not know how low their 1984 results may have been. About two-thirds of the dioceses exceeded their goals, but of course, that raises the question of whether the goals were high or low. The median response rate to the diocesan appeal was fifty percent; one of two prospective donors made a contribution.

Most diocesan campaigns and many parish campaigns are directed and managed by professional fund-raisers who, from my experience, achieve a greater success than do well-intentioned and zealous amateurs. I suspect, however, that professionals have a tendency to set goals rather low so that they will not fail to meet them. Their fees normally (and ethically) are based on the quality and extent of their services, not on a percentage of the donations. A big flop, e.g., failure to reach pre-campaign goals, could ruin a professional fund-raiser's business. Many campaigns, therefore, have goals that are not primarily related to what the diocese or parish needs or to what all its members can afford to contribute, but to the professional's conservative (and self-serving) estimate of the amount that participating Catholics will pledge and donate. Excessively conservative fund-raising goals may have been a large factor in the Church's failure to proclaim courageous objectives based not only on what was needed in terms of *real* dollars but on what Catholics could and would contribute if they were challenged by these same objectives.

Canon law now requires all dioceses and parishes to have financial councils. Their members are expected to be "truly skilled in financial affairs as well as in civil law." Moreover, bishops and pastors are obliged to seek the advice of these councils and to consult with them in depth about diocesan and parochial financial matters.

If I still were an active bishop or a pastor, my first assignment to the financial council would be to do, or to have done, a professional survey of the annual income of all adult members of the diocese or parish. These data are accessible and are used extensively by market research organizations, which always find out how much money people have before they begin to persuade them to buy the products they want to merchandise. The Church should do the same. Before presuming "We can't ask our people for any more money; the only way toward solvency is to reduce expenses," a diocese or a parish ought to find out how much money the people have; whether the amount, in real dollars, is more or less than it was the previous year; and how much a given percentage of people's gross income would yield in church income. This research ought to be done in the name of common sense as well as fiscal responsibility. Of course, I know that all Catholics do not contribute. I also know that there is a big difference between gross and disposable income, that a widow with an income of thirty thousand dollars a year and six children under eighteen cannot afford the same donations as a twenty-six-year-old, unmarried engineer earning thirty-five thousand a year. Market research takes all these factors--and more--into account for its reliable estimates of how a product will sell to a particular income-bracket group.

I am convinced that church leadership (and I, too, beat my breast) does not have a faint or foggy notion of how much money Catholics actually have and how relatively little of it they are donating to the Church. Repeated underestimates of the Church's potential for acquiring funds to meet its needs have caused what I call "the poor mouth syndrome." Repeatedly crying, "We can't afford it," leadership has asked for too little, paid too little to its help, and done far too little to move the great U.S. Catholic Church into the mainstream of American life. In the first part of this book, Father Greeley's data showed Catholics no less generous than Protestants; but they give far less, and I think the reason is that they really do not know how little they actually have been giving.

From top to bottom in the Church there is a need for a change of mind and heart with regard to donations. But one element should not be changed--and that is voluntaryism (a rarely used word but a precisely correct noun signifying the practice of giving freewill, voluntary offerings to churches and charities).

From its very beginning, the Catholic Church in the United States has relied upon voluntary contributions. Unlike much of the Church in Europe, the Church here has not depended upon either government subsidy or use of the government's tax machinery to levy and collect a church tax on its members. This voluntary pattern matched the New World's do-it-yourself spirit, highly prized as a value in America's private sector. Voluntary donations have been and still are a fine expression of generosity. Quite probably, the influence of the Catholic Church in American life and culture would have been far less if its funds had come from the government. Dependent upon the government, the Church would have been hesitant to use the pulpit for constructive criticism of government policies and practices. Moreover, when government pays the bills, citizens feel little obligation to supplement their church taxes by making personal donations.

Because of this tradition of voluntaryism, church authorities have trusted that church members on their honor would contribute generously. Most members have been generous and many still are. To lose this trust and to resort to some kind of compulsion would be bad for the Church, no matter how much additional income it might generate.

The problem with voluntary, generous donations, well motivated by religious convictions, is that they are unpredictable. Not even the donors have a long-range plan for giving. Church authorities can only wait and see what they will have in hand to finance many fixed, certain expenses. Voluntary donations, however generous, usually are spontaneous and impulsive, often running up and down like a yo-yo. That puts administrators in the uncomfortable spot of saying to their employees, "If I knew for sure what would come in during the next twelve months, I would know what I could promise to go out in salaries."

Another difficulty with voluntaryism is that it has led contributors to believe that their donations can reasonably be an amount that they feel like giving, as it were, out of the goodness of their hearts. One hears expressions like the following: "Whenever I go to Mass, I toss something into the basket"; "I had a good day at the races, and Father Pastor will cash in on my good luck"; or "What I put into the basket depends on how I liked the sermon." With income as unpredictable as what horse will win in the seventh at the race track, it is no wonder that some pastors have nervous breakdowns trying to finance a million dollars or more of fixed, inescapable expenses for salaries, utilities, taxes, insurance, etc. In short, voluntaryism has made much of the Church's support a matter of charity.

What is missing most in present patterns of church finance is a sense of justice. Symptoms of this missing link are widely prevalent presumptions such as the following: people who work for the

Church ought to be willing to work for less than they would be paid for comparable work elsewhere; members of a parish or a diocese really are not interested in church budgets (they are available at the rectory or the chancery but whoever asks to see them?); if we ask for any more money there won't be any people in church; and no one can tell people what to give--that's their decision. With justice missing, the Church will continue to poor mouth, to retrench while other enterprises forge ahead, to grub for coins for paying bills in dollar amounts, and to feel sorry for itself.

Let me say emphatically that this inattention to justice's demands is a fault not only of bishops and other administrators. Diocesan and parish pastoral councils and finance councils are also to blame, sometimes being far more pessimistic than the clergy in their forecasts of church income. Top-level attention to justice will not make much difference, however, unless it is joined with a conversion to justice on the part of all those who claim to be members of the Catholic Church.

Justice should persuade everyone in the Church to pay a fair share of parochial and diocesan expenses. Justice does not raise the question "What do I feel like giving as a charitable contribution?" but "What am I obliged to pay, as a fair share related to my income, for the financing of the whole enterprise, all its services to me and to the church community?"

Parishioners, *the people* whose money pays the Church's parochial, diocesan, and institutional bills, are not merely entitled but obliged to have an enlightened understanding of the Church's budgets, especially their parish budget. This presumes, of course, that the parish pastor and the financial council have prepared a budget in accordance with standard accounting procedures, have appended to it full explanations of the *raison d' etre* of all major expenditures, and have indicated a range of percentages of gross income which all parishioners will be expected to pay toward a balanced parish budget. This budget, however, should not be a document secretly put together in rectory privacy and then mailed to parishioners as a *fait accompli*. After a preliminary budget is prepared by the finance council and approved by a formal resolution of the parish pastoral council, it should be distributed by mail or as a supplement to the parish Sunday bulletin. Thereafter, parishioners should be invited and encouraged to come to one of half a dozen or more budget hearings scheduled at various times for parishioners' convenience. After the budget is revised in light of parishioners' requests and wishes, it should again be submitted to them for a vote-- preferably by mailed ballots or at least by ballots available at Sunday Masses.

By this method or a similar method, parishioners can be persuaded that the parish budget, both its expenditures and income, is *their* budget, which they must keep balanced by donating their fair share of parish income. Pastors, therefore, must insist that the budget is not simply for parishioners' information but calls for their participation in the parish enterprise.

I see much merit, and I have alluded to this previously, in encouraging parishioners to pledge a fixed percentage of their gross income for their total annual donation to the Church. In a single year or over a span of several years, parishioners' gross income may go up or down (usually up!); corresponding adjustments of their donations to the Church would be a matter of honor. For those distressed by a severe reduction of their personal income, a smaller donation to the Church would cause no guilt. From my experience, I feel that donors usually are frightened by large numbers, such as eight hundred dollars a year or fifteen a week. Asked for two percent of an annual gross income of forty thousand dollars, a parishioner might not be so alarmed, but the end cash result would be the same.

I advocate a range of one to three percent, perhaps as high as four percent in some places. Some donors, because of other obligations such as their children's Catholic college education, care of aged parents, and extraordinary medical bills, can opt for the minimum of one percent (one tenth of a tithe). At the same time, those with few extraordinary obligations or those with deep faith that generous giving is a blessed way to worship can choose the upper percentage of three or four or more. Most, I think, would choose two percent, including those already laying out ten or more percent of their income for Catholic schooling of their children (their parents, Father Greeley's work shows, are most generous contributors). Incidentally, if *all* parishioners were to contribute two to three percent of their gross income, many parishes with schools probably could increase their school subsidies substantially. They would then be able to raise teachers' salaries without having to push tuition and fees, particularly in high schools, to a dangerous point of no return (i.e., fewer new students and a decline in the number of students presently enrolled).

Although I do not have data to prove it, I am reasonably sure that a typical middle-income parish with a school would be in good to excellent financial condition if its annual income, exclusive of tuition and fees, were an amount equal to two percent of all parishioners' gross income. The perplexing, enormous difficulty, however, is that, in the typical parish, sixty percent or more of its income-earning adults presently are contributing little or nothing. The rule of thumb is that twenty percent of the parishioners pay eighty percent of the expenses, school tuition excluded. This terrible situation screams for immediate and radical correction. What's wrong and what can be done about it? There is no one, simple answer, other than to say that *something* must be done and if it is, then there will be at least a little improvement.

What's wrong? Personally, I am well aware of a parochial predicament not uncommon in many city parishes. For eleven years, I was pastor of a Chicago parish that had, I guessed, about eight thousand baptized Roman Catholics over the age of eighteen resident within its boundaries who, if asked for the name of their parish, would have replied, "St. Ferdinand's." I would estimate that, on Sundays, about fifty-five hundred adults attended one of eleven Masses celebrated in the church or the overflow chapel. They came to worship, to drop off their Sunday envelopes, and to buy the Sunday newspapers. Within the parish were its own parochial school enrolling about one thousand pupils, two Catholic high schools enrolling three thousand adolescents, and a secular hospital with at least two hundred Catholic patients in need of sacramental ministry. Engulfed, swamped, overwhelmed by this mass of active Catholics all over the place, I did not bother with a census (we could not take care of those we had; why look for more?), nor did I hustle for more money (the parish had a million on deposit with the chancery). People kept coming in droves Sunday after Sunday. Every year they stepped up their donations, even enough to give substantial help to an impoverished inner-city parish. My breathless schedule went on and on until I resigned, perfectly willing to let a new administrator keep on top of the whole thing.

The wrong and sad side of all this is that thousands of lost sheep (not much aware of how lost they were) were neglected and hundreds of freeloaders, those who contributed little or nothing to the parish, were not called to task.

What can be done in similar difficulties? First and foremost, the whole parish--not only the pastor, his associate pastors, and staff--has to realize profoundly that *all* baptized Roman Catholics are members of the parish community, excepting those who formally have joined other denominations or who flatly declare: "I don't belong to the Church anymore." Parish membership is not restricted to those who are registered and/or use Sunday envelopes. No longer, I believe, should attendance at Sunday Mass be the single criterion of active Catholicism; evidence is mounting that some Catholics negligent about Sunday Mass are otherwise exceptionally virtuous and even "church-minded" in other respects, while some Mass-going Catholics still equate being Catholic with fulfillment of that one regulation.

People who *de facto* belong to a parish, who expect its services when necessary or desirable, and who receive many unseen benefits--e.g., remembrance at Mass and abundant graces flowing around in the parish community--have to be made to understand and feel that their membership is a reality where it matters most: in the sight of God. These people, supposedly on the edge of the parish because they are not often seen around the parish church, should be urged to study the parish budget and like other parishioners and to cast their votes for or against it. They, too, should be asked to pledge a percentage of their income and should be assured that, if they wish, their payments can be made by mail in response to monthly reminders from the parish office.

And who is going to make an approach to these "fringe" parishioners? Obviously, the pastor alone cannot do it all. The management of its complexities might even be too much to ask of him. In a typical city parish, hundreds of volunteers will be needed to undertake a persistent, unwearied, gentle, and intelligent approach to every adult Catholic obliged to financial support of the parish. A ratio of one to twenty would be necessary--one volunteer to each twenty adults, active and fringe. Of course, all volunteers would have to go through a comprehensive educational program. This program would cover a review of contemporary ecclesiology; techniques in dealing with such extremes as hyper-enthusiasm, cynicism, hostility, resentment, etc.; and an in-depth study of the parish's projects and corresponding budgets. Appropriate prayer and reflection would also be incorporated into the educational program. A graduation exercise might include the volunteers' own pledges of a percentage of their income. Clergy and religious should participate in this pledge ceremony as well. (Yes, I did say that. As Protestant ministers do, priests and sisters should pledge a percentage of their income, vow of poverty notwithstanding, to their parish.)

Parishes may be hesitant about approaching alienated Catholics with a rather insistent request for pledged donations. There is indeed a danger that some lapsed or fallen-away Catholics, particularly those bitterly alienated because of actual or suspected mismanagement of church funds, may slam the door and, in their words, "leave the Church for good." Others may be upset that the Church's very first encounter with them since they became alienated is a hard sell for money. However, there are numerous Catholics who, although rather distant from the church of their youth--and not missing it much--may react favorably to a layperson's solicitude for their well-being. They may be kindly disposed toward pledging a regular donation even while they continue their search for a prodigal's way home. Research on alienated and/or inactive Catholics indicates that the majority by far have not apostatized and joined another religion; they have only drifted away from an institutional religion about which they have some bad memories and toward which they no longer feel much attraction. But that need not mean that they want to be freeloaders.

Paradoxical traits in the American psyche are a dislike for cheaters and an urge to cheat. We dislike freeloaders--people who cheat in business, on their taxes, on welfare, or on whatever they can-- but still, we have an urge to get away with something if we can, not to be a chump and pay for something that might be free, or to let someone else bear the burden. When soliciting funds, parish visitors have to be diplomatic about helping freeloaders realize that they are cheating, and on something sacred--their duty to support their church.

My suggestions, I admit, may be difficult to put into practice. Parishioners willing to go door to door in quest of parish support are hard to find. Maintaining momentum for this kind of drive calls for enormous pastoral energy in the rectory. The whole thing will collapse of its own weight if, at the same time that it is undertaken, parish services are not improved and then perceived as much better by most parishioners. Blending persistence and patience is not easy. Nonetheless, the present common practice of letting thirty percent of the parishioners bear virtually the full burden of financing a parish is both unjust and shortsighted. To instill a sense of justice in all parishioners is now a paramount pastoral responsibility. No longer can the Church hope to be just to its employees (underpaying a church employee "cries to heaven for vengeance") and to finance its ministries in a post-Vatican II era without the sense of justice being a pervasive value in the whole Church.

Some may object that my plan will project an image of the Church as a sort of social club exacting dues from all its members (pay or get out) instead of as a true servant, like Jesus Christ, "not to be served but to serve." A further objection is that some people may try to buy heaven by donating money to a parish church they rarely attend. "Tainted money," a friend has said to me, "ultimately will curse the Church."

The only pastoral answer to these objections is a parish's solicitude for the *full* spiritual welfare of those parishioners who care at least enough to make a donation. To get their money and settle for that would be utterly unworthy of a parish calling itself Catholic.

When a parish intends to seek support from all its adult members, it probably should take a hard look at the ways it collects pledged payments. Baskets pushed around or passed around during the Sunday liturgies is a questionable practice. It seems to suggest that only churchgoers are expected to contribute. Furthermore, it perpetuates the false and inept idea, still dominant in many Catholic minds, that tossing a donation--any old amount-- into the basket is a rational way to support the parish and its diocese. What happens far too often is that many Catholics toss in donations far less than they owe in justice and far less than they can afford.

The collection basket has other faults, notably that only envelope users, normally the father of a family, generally drop anything into it. Adolescents and children, seeming to slip into a momentary ecstasy, do not even see the basket passed before them. In many parishes, venerable ushers--some of whom have not participated actively in a full Sunday Mass for years--irritate the congregation by pushing baskets as though they were out trapping rats! If there must be pushed baskets (enlightened parishes trust their parishioners to pass the offertory baskets from pew to pew), the pushers might well be attractive young men and women capable of a smile while they perform their task. (This reference to men and women ushers is the only sex in *this* book!)

Now that the computer age has arrived and is becoming increasingly pervasive, it may also be time to examine the use of computer technology for assessing and collecting the fair shares that adult Catholics owe their church. Many families and single adults with their own income might be willing, even well disposed, to be billed for the amount of money which they have pledged for their fair share (Protestants call this "donation notification!"). This procedure might be less costly and more efficient than Sunday envelopes. I hasten to remark, however, that, initially, parishioners should be given a choice of the traditional Sunday envelope or a monthly notification.

Not wanting for a moment to separate donations to the Church from the Eucharist and from the Offertory of the Mass, I will later on in this book express my views on making a much closer connection.

In summary, I believe that church support is an obligation in justice incumbent upon all baptized Catholics. I think that the Church should urge justice as the prime motive for donations. The

Church's plan for just donations should call for a fair share related to an individual's income. All fair-share persons are entitled, as though they were shareholders, to a participating role in the allocation and expenditure of their investment and to a full report from management on income and expenditures in a parish and diocese. All this efficiency, however, should be tempered, as necessary, to preserve the priceless value of voluntary giving.

2.4 / CHARITY

AND ALMS

My forceful advocacy of justice as a prime motive for honest, fair, reliable support of the institutional church need not and does not denigrate the sound value of almsgiving, an essential element of authentic Christian living. When U.S. Catholics are invited to give alms, they usually are extraordinarily generous and cheerful givers and make little fuss about it. In giving alms, Catholics are true to Jesus' admonition not to let one hand know what the other is doing.

More often than not, the most generous alms are spontaneous--an immediate, unplanned, and unrecorded donation to people ravaged by a calamity like famine or earthquake. Such appeals for alms draw greater generosity than do perennial campaigns for Catholic Relief Services, Human Development, Propagation of the Faith, and Catholic Charities.

While I was bishop of Fort Wayne-South Bend, I made a sudden appeal for food for starving people in Ethiopia whose plight had been graphically publicized in TV specials. At all Sunday Masses, the faithful heard my on-the-spot request for all their loose change--all their coins, no bills unless they wanted to give them. Approximately sixty thousand dollars *in coins* were collected from about seventy thousand adults (over fourteen) at Masses in eighty-five churches. If similar "give all your change for alms" collections were taken up every Sunday in my former diocese, the total for a year would be at least three million dollars, all in coins. The point here is quite clear to me. In the Fort Wayne-South Bend diocese, it should be easy (but it has not been) to raise three million dollars in alms for charitable causes. The amount actually raised was far less, and the reason, I must humbly admit, is that I did not have the wit, energy, and "go out and get it" spirit necessary to collect the alms available for the asking. If, every Sunday, all adult Catholics attending Mass in U.S. churches were to donate all the loose change in their pockets and purses, the estimated annual yield (my estimate) of alms for the poor would be five hundred million dollars a year.

The Church's problem is not that Catholics do not have money to give or that they are selfish or that they have little faith in the eternal value of almsgiving. Rather, the problem is that the Church's routine collection procedures have blurred the distinction between church support and almsgiving--to the detriment of both.

Hundreds of times I have seen this confusion at Sunday liturgies. During the Offertory of the Mass, ushers take up the collection of envelopes and loose money to pay the parish expenses. That should be the time of the Mass when gifts, alms, and donations with no strings should be collected. Many parishioners presume, however, that their envelopes for church support are alms, and many of those who put nothing in the basket assume that "Daddy has taken care of it." About once a month, there is a special collection for some charitable cause, usually taken up after the Offertory is finished or at the end of Mass. Parishioners who deposited their envelopes in the first collection let the basket pass them by; "We already made our donation," they reason.

The most deplorable result of this liturgically inept practice is that few people at Mass have even a vague idea why and how their almsgiving is an integral component of their liturgical worship. Not a word of prayer accompanies their donations. There is little or no awareness that, in return for their Offertory gift, God will nourish them with the precious gift of Jesus' Body and Blood in the Eucharist. They give little attention to the Eucharist's essential reciprocity: "What shall I render to the Lord in return for all He has done for me?" The people in the pews are not at fault. Most probably, many never have heard a clear explanation of the Offertory, a part of the Mass in which they should be playing a prominent role.

A little ingenuity and wit would correct this situation easily. At every Sunday Mass in a typical parish with a stable, in-residence population, the Offertory should be designed to give all in the congregation a religious experience of almsgiving. The prayers of the faithful at Mass should set the mood. They should not be the canned pabulum peddled by weary publishers of missalettes but should be carefully prepared and phrased as prayers for the beneficiaries of the alms to be gathered. The presiding priest should explain, in one minute, the cause or causes to which all the alms will be donated. The congregation should be given time to reflect prayerfully on the amount of a donation they want to give. While an appropriate hymn is sung, donations of alms from everyone, ages three to one hundred, should be gathered in many baskets expeditiously passed around the church. Previous instruction in bulletins and sermons should have explained why a donation, even if it is only a penny, is made by all. Placing a gift in the offertory basket would become as habitual as genuflecting or taking holy water (but hopefully more prayerful). Parishioners who wished to deposit their church support envelope could do so at the same time; the envelope, however, would be in addition to their alms.

My suggested procedure is open to a myriad of local adaptations. But however it is done, it will, I feel sure, make a distinction between, on the one hand, support of the Church in justice and, on the other, almsgiving in charity focused on the Eucharist. I venture the opinion that a parish that has made almsgiving into a vital religious experience for its members will have little difficulty obtaining adequate support for its ministries.

2.5 / THE BISHOPS LETTER ON

THE ECONOMY

The Church's urgent need for justice in the management of its own finances has been underscored by unprecedented declarations in a document published by the National Conference of Catholic Bishops. Five years in production, it was formally approved November 13, 1986, by a vote of two hundred and twenty-nine to nine. Its title is: *Economic Justice for All: Catholic Social Teaching and the U.S. Economy*, but it is popularly called "the bishops letter on the U.S. economy."

Before I comment on the statements in the letter about justice in the Church itself, I must note that, though bishops are its authors, it accurately reflects insights they gained from extensive consultation with the people of God. This accurate reflection includes a rather dim awareness of the financial consequences inseparable from the letter's assertions about justice in the Church. The pastoral letter, however, is a fact, and now the whole Church, not bishops alone, has the duty to implement its own just ideals and standards, specifically for its thousands of salaried employees. The cost will require substantially increased income.

All those in dioceses, parishes, and institutions who are responsible for finances would be well advised, while and after reading the pastoral, to make a meditation on Matthew 23:1-4, which reads: "Then addressing the people and His disciples, Jesus said, 'The scribes and the Pharisees occupy the chair of Moses. You must do, therefore, what they tell you and listen to what they say, but do not be guided by what they do since they do not practice what they preach. They tie up heavy burdens and lay them on men's shoulders, but will they lift a finger to move them? Not they!'" No matter whether the pastoral letter impacts the U.S. economy or becomes only a curious little essay read by a few persons studying social ethics, its practical credibility will depend much on the extent to which the whole Church at least tries to practice what it has preached.

With italicized emphasis, the letter says: "All the moral principles that govern the just operation of any economic endeavor apply to the church and its agencies and institutions; indeed, the church should be exemplary."

That's a mouthful! Much to my surprise, the word "exemplary" was neither challenged nor questioned during the extended discussion and debate on the pastoral; this makes me wonder whether the bishops had thought much about its consequences back home in their dioceses. Perhaps the reason is that the letter's specifics for exemplary justice in the Church are considerably less clear than are its detailed recommendations for the economy in general.

The letter's section on justice in the Church addresses five areas: (1) wages and salaries, (2) rights of employees, (3) investments and property, (4) works of charity, and (5) working for economic justice. The area of most immediate concern for this book is "wages and salaries," an area directly related to the need for vastly increased church income.

On wages and salaries, the letter says: "We bishops commit ourselves to the principle that those who serve the church--laity, clergy and reli-

gious--should receive a sufficient livelihood and social benefits provided by responsible employers in
our nation."

Earnest and courageous though this commitment may be, it does not give church employees
a clear idea of what the Church will pay in dollars
and cents for "sufficient livelihood." Will a married
woman employed as a Catholic school teacher be
told that eleven thousand dollars a year is sufficient
livelihood because it is second income for her family? Will a priest be told that three hundred dollars
a month in salary is sufficient livelihood for a celibate male when it is added to free rectory room and
board and a few other perks? Is sufficient livelihood for a Sister with a vow of poverty to be com-
puted as less than what is needed by an unmarried
lay teacher?

In my opinion, the pastoral letter's definition
of a just wage for church employees falls short of
being "exemplary." It leaves too much room for
church officials and their lay committees to fall
back on false presumptions, e.g., people who work
for the Church should be willing to sacrifice, should
not expect the Church to pay the high wages paid to
others in similar or identical professions, should be
paid only what the Church's contributors are willing
to donate for salaries, etc. Canonical minds may
discover too many loopholes in this ambiguous criterion of "sufficient livelihood."

If the bishops candidly had acknowledged
that many church employees now are being paid
dreadfully low (far from exemplary) wages and
salaries, then they would, of necessity, have been
much more specific about the practical components

of a just wage. It was the bishops' close attention to specific data about the plight of persons on public welfare which motivated the specificity of their proposals for welfare reform.

Though I claim no particular competence in social ethics, I believe that there must be a better and more specific criterion than "sufficient livelihood" to determine a just wage for a church employee. Perhaps a reasonable standard might be the average salary income of Catholics who foot the bills for their church employees' salaries. Specifically, this would mean, for example, that Catholic school teachers would be paid a monthly salary equal to the average salary paid to Catholics who have a college degree and hold professional positions. If, in a given geographical area, the average monthly salary paid to a Catholic graduate from college were sixteen hundred, then a Catholic school teacher would start at the same monthly rate. The same criterion would hold for upward adjustments. The premise for this proposal is that, on the average, Catholics can afford to pay a church employee a salary that is an average of their own salaries, adjustments being made for variations related to college degrees, experience, and type of work in which the church employee is engaged. Simply stated, the principle is an application of "do unto others as you would have them do unto you," i.e., what Catholics earn should be a large factor in determining the amount of salary that they, *the Church*, should pay.

Some limited consultation with a few chief Catholic school administrators has persuaded me that, "exemplary" though my proposed criterion may be, it is not likely to catch on because of its complexity, notably the factor of the average income earned by Catholics holding a college degree in a given employment area. The administrators seem to prefer a salary scale for Catholic school teachers based on a percentage (always less!) of the amount paid public school teachers in the area. While acknowledging the administrators' best of intentions, I have serious reservations about both the justice and wisdom of a scale that pays less than what is paid to public school teachers, who, as professions go, are themselves in a low-paying occupation. Fixing Catholic school salaries at rates less than public school rates disregards even questioning whether the Church can afford to pay equal or more than public school teachers earn.

Several weeks of conversation and reflection on the salary question, now a hot topic in many dioceses and parishes working on the next fiscal year's budget, have brought me to six specific conclusions. Here they are:

(1)In Catholic hospitals, social service agencies, and most chancery offices and tribunals, many employees are receiving a just wage. Hospital and social service agencies have help from government and community sources. If Catholic schools were receiving the public aid that they deserve, then, like Catholic schools in some nearby provinces of Canada, they, too, would be paying their teachers a just wage. There should be much more shouting that Catholic school teachers are getting a raw deal because the state and federal governments give the schools a bad deal.

(2)For the foreseeable future, Catholic school teaching will be a low-paying job; so will public school teaching. It should be presumed, therefore, that persons entering and remaining in the teaching profession realize that their pay always will be low, to be compensated at least in part by some non-monetary values in the profession.

(3)The evil clamoring for immediate attention and correction with all due haste is the *underpayment* of thousands of Catholic school teachers, i.e., paying salaries far less than what the Church could afford if it undertook a realignment of its finances (cross-financing between parishes, for example) and raised the additional money Catholics can afford to pay for just salaries. The responsibility for just wages in the schools rests with the whole Church, not only with parents. Whether a school is a winner or a loser should not be determined by whether it operates in the black or in the red when left to itself but by whether it has both a short-term and long-term impact on its students' Christian development. Having declared dozens of times that Catholic schools are "ideal" for the education of the young, bishops should rely even more than they do now on the support of the whole Church for this "ideal."

(4) I think that the *minimum* starting salary for any church employed professional holding a college degree and otherwise qualified and certified should be four hundred dollars a week. That is about the present starting wage for Catholic hospital nurses and Catholic social service case workers. The minimum salary for experienced professional employees, presumably retained year after year for their satisfactory and meritorious service, ought to be five percent over the base four hundred dollars a week for each full year of employment. The minimum wage for a ten-year employee, therefore, would be six hundred dollars a week.

The intricate question about how many weeks in a year a teacher should be employed and should be paid is too large and complex for me even to suggest an answer at this time. The question involves the number of weeks children in an industrial society ought to be in school, the extent to which teachers are improving themselves professionally throughout the year, whether the nine-month year is one of the main attractions of school teaching, etc. An attempt to raise all teachers to my proposed minimum weekly salary would be enough for a typical diocese or parish to undertake over a period of the next one to three years. These minimums for all professionals are, I believe, affordable in light of evidence in the first part of this book.

(5) My proposed minimum for paraprofessionals, semiprofessionals, and others employed full time is three hundred a week, with a five percent increase on base for each year of service.

(6) The National Conference of Catholic Bishops (NCCB), mindful that its pastoral on the economy has advocated enforcement and extension of our nation's minimum wage laws, should formally adopt a *recommendation* (that is as far as NCCB is authorized to go) that, effective fiscal 1989, the minimum starting wage for professionals would be four hundred dollars a week and for nonprofessionals, three hundred a week.

Candor makes me admit that some of my friends' reactions to my proposals have been outrage and indignation. Some pastors have ridiculed the plan as utter nonsense--"asking parishioners to increase their donations twenty-five percent or more just to give school teachers more money!" Others say: "It won't work; people are not going to give that kind of money for salaries." One of the nation's best informed and most successful development directors says that big business will be inclined to contribute to Catholic schools only as long as they follow business rules--i.e., only pay teachers the going market rate for qualified, competent personnel, following the law of supply and demand.

Another friend warned: "Your proposed NCCB resolution effectively would close down most Catholic schools by the turn of the century." Another critic suggested: "Why don't you *really* retire and keep quiet?!"

Undaunted, I stand by the heart of my position that church employees should be paid wages approximately equal to the average income of the church's members in similar occupational categories. Perhaps my proposed rates may turn out to be faulty--too high or too low--in light of future research (research that NCCB ought to be undertaking to give credence to its own economic recommendations for the Church as "an economic actor"). But I would be willing to guess, even bet, that my figures as they stand are very close to being correct.

"This obligation" (i.e., just compensation for church employees), the bishops pastoral says about as timidly as possible, "cannot be met without increased contributions of all members of the Church." That is jejune language to say the obvious. Unfortunately, far too many people will read into it a dismal prediction that just salaries will not be paid because Catholics, given their track record since they moved into upper- and middle-income brackets, are not likely to increase their contributions beyond the rate of inflation. Therefore, the pastoral's teaching runs the risk of being dismissed by many Catholics as high-minded, well-intentioned, wishful thinking.

The pastoral letter would be much more persuasive, even convincing, if immediately after its statement about funding, it said plainly: "And there is abundant evidence on hand to assure us that the Church, i.e., all its members, can afford to pay just salaries without neglect or compromise of other financial responsibilities." Instead, the pastoral says: "Sacrificial giving or tithing by all people of God would provide the funds necessary to pay these adequate salaries for religious and lay people; the lack of funds is the usual underlying cause for lack of adequate salaries for religious and lay people."

Data in the first part of this book, far from making a case for "sacrificial giving or tithing," clearly show that an honest, reasonable sharing of the institutional church's expenses is what is needed for adequate salaries. If all salaried Catholics paid two to three percent of their salary income for the support of their parish and diocese, the Church would have more than enough to pay all employees adequate salaries and benefits. To propose that "all" Catholics tithe to finance church expenses is utterly utopian; few people are going to leap from 1.1% giving to 10.0% giving.

The pastoral declares: "The obligation to sustain the Church's institutions--education and health care, social services agencies, religious education programs, care of the elderly, youth ministry and the like--falls on all the members of the community because of their baptism; the obligation is not just on the users or those who staff them." While I would not question the statement's main thrust that all baptized Catholics are obliged to pay a fair share of their church's expenses, I find its ecclesiology rather strange: Catholics are obliged to contribute to the Church "because of their baptism," and there is, I infer, some kind of a distinction between "users" and "non-users."

Why be so complicated? Of course, baptism makes a person a member of the Church. All members, however, are "users," at least in the sense that this membership incorporates them into the Mystical Body of Christ from which they derive spiritual benefits. The plain fact of justice (the virtue which dictates giving to another whatever is due) is that all people who belong to the Church have an obligation to support it. I really do not think that one of the effects of baptism is use of the Sunday envelopes.

I fear that many readers of the bishops letter will summarize its various assertions by saying that *if* the Church can raise the necessary funds, *then* it ought to pay its employees a just wage. That is a contingent rather than a committed way to go about it. Pastors, for example, will tell their people, "If you increase your Sunday donations by twenty-five to fifty percent, then the parish will pass along all the increased income to parish employees--giving them a twenty to thirty percent raise. If, however, you do not increase your Sunday offerings, then the parish will have to ask its employees to continue working for low wages."

That approach, which many pastors would call "realistic," actually will be, in many instances, hopeless. It offers parishioners a choice: pay low wages or high wages--it's up to you--as though the option either way is defensible. It also ignores the fact that some people with a lot of money may have it because they successfully have paid low wages to their employees. "Why," these affluent individuals will ask, "pay higher salaries to church employees who, anyway, ought to be willing to make a sacrifice?"

This optional route is not the road that pastors follow in their requests for more money to pay increased utility bills, higher insurance costs, or necessary repairs. For these items, the approach is that these parish expenses are going up and the parish, therefore, *must* have increased donations to pay its bills. Everyone understands, of course; the electric bill *must* be paid even though it has gone up fifteen percent and the parking lot *must* be repaired even though it will cost thirty thousand dollars. This same approach should be made for salaries. The pastor should announce that after consultation with the parish's finance committee and the parish council, he has come to the conclusion that salaries *must* be raised twenty-five percent. And the parish *must* receive enough additional income to pay them. There are no options; the money *must* come in. And I think it *will*, because the people have it to give.

In the area of "rights of employees," the bishops letter declares that "all church institutions must fully recognize the rights of employees to organize and bargain collectively with the institution through whatever association or organization they freely choose." This declaration will become much more operative when Catholic Church institutions, though exempt (for protection of their tax exempt status) from the jurisdiction of the National Labor Relations Board, voluntarily follow all applicable NLRB rules and procedures. Catholic Church employees should be promised the full equivalent of

NLRB protection when they engage in collective bargaining. Beyond that, the NCCB should develop some clear, encouraging guidelines to help all church institutions with the development of exemplary patterns of management-labor collaboration. Merely to assert that church employees have the right to unionize falls far short of encouraging them to do so. Without this encouragement, most church employees probably will continue to hope for the best in personal, individual negotiations with their employers.

To protect their tax exempt status, church institutions are also exempt from federal laws protecting employees' vested pension rights. Endeavoring to be exemplary, the NCCB should therefore adopt a policy or approve a study which, in effect, would call upon all church institutions to give employees the same pension protection they would have if they were employed by a corporation under the jurisdiction of federal law. As it now stands, a church institution can wipe out all pension benefits for an employee who is discharged or who quits before becoming eligible for pension. Some priests who left the active ministry after many years of service have lost all their diocesan pension. Church authorities assert that no injustice was done because the priest's pension was noncontributory (i.e., the priest paid nothing). That assertion, however, ignores the obvious fact that the noncontributory pension was a form of compensation, not a gift. It also ignores the fact that an employee covered by federal law has vested pension rights after ten years of employment even though the pension is noncontributory.

These two situations highlight the need for a church policy to guarantee and to protect church employees' benefits so that church employees' could enjoy the same assurance they would have if their benefits were regulated by law.

Another situation irritating diocesan priests is that social security regulations classify a priest as "self-employed" (at the behest of the bishops conference's plea for protection of tax exemption). Consequently, he has to pay both the employer's and employee's social security tax, close to fourteen percent of his income. Priests who have promised "to obey" their bishop do not feel that they are self-employed. This fiction costs them dearly when they pay their social security tax.

Commendably, the bishops letter urges that the nation's tax system "should be structured according to the principle of progressivity, so that those with relatively greater financial resources pay a higher rate of taxation." Ignoring this recommendation within its own structure, the NCCB again this year levied a flat, nonprogressive tax on all dioceses. For Bridgeport, Connecticut, a diocese with thousands of high-income families and for Gallup, New Mexico, a diocese with thousands of residents with incomes below the poverty level, the NCCB tax was a flat 13.3 cents per person, i.e., anyone counted by the diocese as a baptized Roman Catholic. The way dioceses count is quite arbitrary. Some use accurate data from a complete diocesan census. Others make a good guess based on the pastors' guesses of their parishes' Catholic population. Obviously, a reform of NCCB's taxing procedures is imperative in light of its own moral stance on government taxes.

The NCCB's archaic and unjust tax system is one reason why the organization repeatedly gets into a fuss about high costs, reduced expenditures, and other penny-pinching antics. The organization is sadly underfunded with the result that the Church is ill served by inadequately financed programs. NCCB's neglect of research, particularly research in the area of religious sociology, has left it open to a charge of "the blind leading the blind into the pit."

Tucked away in the bishops letter is a promise that will cost millions and is, of itself, a salutary reason for launching fund-raising efforts with unprecedented, high goals. Setting forth remedies for terrible poverty still prevalent in a rich nation, the bishops wisely commend inner-city Catholic schools for their "well merited reputation of providing excellent education, especially for the poor." "These schools," the bishops say, "provide an effective vehicle for disadvantaged students to lift themselves out of poverty. . . . *We pledge ourselves to continue the effort to make Catholic schools models of education for the poor.*" (Italics mine.)

Presuming that the bishops were not indulging in escapist rhetoric that might get them off the hook from their commitment to Catholic inner-city schools, I feel safe in saying that the bishops have declared plainly that they are going to keep open all inner-city Catholic schools for which there are poor children in need of this high quality education. I see nothing contingent in the bishops' statement. It does not say, "if we have the money," or "if we can repair the old buildings," or "if we can fund the teachers," or "if these children are Catholic." The word "pledge" was carefully chosen, and I take it to mean an honest, sincere promise to have an even stronger presence of Catholic school education in the inner city.

The expense of this pledge will be enormous, beyond my prediction with the data of which I am aware. Nevertheless, I am convinced that the evidence in the first part of this book will not tolerate any compromise of the U.S. bishops' solemn pledge on the score that American Catholics cannot afford it. In fact, the inner city is where their contributions can best be expended; that is where the contributions belong. I do not hesitate to say it is where the Lord Jesus Christ wants them to be.

I foresee much pastoral pain for bishops and their close associates who pick up the heavy cross of begging for millions of dollars more to finance an increasingly expensive institutional church eager to be not only an efficient organization but a dedicated servant. Like the Lord Himself on His *Via Dolorosa*, bishops will need many Simons to help them carry the cross. Thousands and thousands of Catholic laity need only be asked.

2.6 / SIGNS OF HOPE

Even those Catholics who complain about too much authoritarianism in the Church like to know what the Church's official position is-- whether they agree or not. Moreover, in due time, Catholics do take seriously those pronouncements of the Church which, though difficult, are rooted in sound theology developed out of the Bible and tradition.

There is no dearth of official pronouncements about justice in the Church. There is not much new or startling to add to what the Church officially has been teaching since Vatican II.

Twenty years ago, in a major document, *The Church in Our Day*, the U.S. bishops courageously declared: "The Church has addressed itself to social justice. . . . If Catholic performance does not match Catholic promise, then truly we shall have failed." Four years later, at the Second Synod of Bishops in Rome, the U.S. delegates supported a synodal decree, a landmark for justice in the Church: "While the Church is bound to give witness to justice she recognizes that anyone who ventures to speak to people about justice must first be just in their own eyes. Hence we must undertake an examination of the modes of acting and of possessions and of life-style found within the Church itself. . . . Those who serve the Church by their labor, including priests and religious, should receive a sufficient livelihood and enjoy the social security which is customary in their region." Perhaps "sufficient livelihood" is about the best criterion to which a worldwide synod could agree. Nevertheless, I think that the U.S. bishops should have done more in their economic pastoral than just borrow it; as I have argued previously, they should have been more specific.

The revised code of canon law, fifteen years in the making, advocates cross-funding within and between dioceses and declares clearly: "Lay persons have a right to decent remuneration suited to their condition; by such remuneration they should be able to provide decently for their own needs and for those of their family."

In 1982, Rome's Sacred Congregation for Catholic Education published an official document entitled *Lay Catholics in Schools: Witness to Faith.* It is a remarkably forthright call for justice: "If the directors of a school and the lay people who work in the school are to live according to the same ideals, two things are essential. First, lay people must receive an adequate salary, guaranteed by a well defined contract, for the work they do in the school: a salary that will permit them to live in dignity, without excessive work or need for additional employment that will interfere with the duties of an educator. This may not be immediately possible without putting an enormous financial burden on the families, or making the school so expensive that it becomes a school for a small elite group; but so long as a truly adequate salary is not being paid, the laity should see in the school directors a genuine preoccupation to find the resources necessary to achieve this end. Second, laity should participate authentically in the responsibility for the school; this assumes they have the ability that is needed in all areas and are sincerely committed to the educational objectives that characterize a Catholic school."

Though the bishops letter on the economy has several limitations, about which I have commented rather sharply, it is truly a prophetic document, one which forty years earlier in 1947, when I was a staffer for the bishops conference in Washington, I would have thought to have been utterly impossible. At that time, I once was severely reprimanded for aiding and abetting my secretary's efforts to start an employees' union. Challenged, I was asked to reveal what I knew about "secret meetings in the women's restroom!" "We've come a long way, Virginia!"

One other document, never much publicized, merits a quotation. Entitled *Precepts of Stewardship*, it was produced and approved in 1977 by three conferences--the bishops conference, the top officers of religious orders of men, and the leadership of women religious. Its preamble is a fairly good endorsement of authentic stewardship programs now catching on in some dioceses and parishes: "Christian stewardship is the practical realization that everything we have is a gift from God. . . . For men and women especially committed to building up the kingdom of God, stewardship heightens an awareness of responsibilities in matters of material concern no less than in spiritual endeavor. . . . Requests for money besides being truthful and forthright must be made on a theologically sound basis and should always be in good taste to strive to lift the hearts and minds of men and women to a greater love of God and neighbors."

Without the slightest disparagement of Christian stewardship, an idea and plan for which I have both admiration and emotional attachment, I think that my little review of church documentation definitely shows that the immediate imperative is justice in the Church. This justice must be implemented by *all* members, not only by those who, bless them, have achieved the conversion of mind and heart to motivate their giving not in terms of what the institutional church needs but in terms of gratitude to God for all He has given. Here, I will remark that if I were starting a new parish or a new diocese, my Act I would be stewardship, the long-haul route to justice and charity. But underpaid employees should not be asked to await massive *metanoia* in the Catholic community; and that is why I urge a sense of justice in the Church as a pressing imperative for action.

Another hopeful sign is a number of movements to narrow the gap between the Church's teaching on justice and the pastoral practices in dioceses and parishes.

Energetic fund-raisers like to position their multiple and varied activities within the category of "development"--somewhat of a buzz word these days. Development, rather crudely defined, simply means a plan to draw upon every conceivable resource for the funding of church activities and projects. It represents a break from overdependence upon the people in the pews and a shift to appeals for large donations from affluent Catholics and from foundations, corporations, and other individuals. "Planned giving" encourages contributors to include the Church in bequests, memorials, and insurance.

Many development projects are pointed toward endowment, thus to end hand-to-mouth financing of stable church enterprises. The National Catholic Development Conference and the Development Department of the National Catholic Educational Association arrange well-planned forums to exchange ideas on development. The leaders of this development movement include able and experienced individuals like Father John A. Flynn of Omaha, Nebraska. Hopefully, they will add a large measure of intelligence and grace to fund-raising that, in the hands of some professionals, produced a lot of money but a horrible image of the Church. I do not blame these professionals; though eager to do a good job for the Church, they had scant direction on how to go about it without making the Church look like its god was the almighty dollar.

Christian stewardship under Catholic auspices is growing. This year, the National Catholic Stewardship Council is celebrating its twenty-fifth anniversary. Mr. Amato A. Semenza, its executive director, told me that bishops and pastors are weary of pounding their people year after year and month after month with appeals to finance dozens of worthy causes. They are tired of always worrying whether their appeals will succeed or fail and of really seeing no light at the end of the tunnel. They are now looking for in-depth, long-term ways to stabilize income by relating it not to each and every need but to an amount of money which Catholics *in faith* believe that they should return to God in gratitude for all He has done for them. According to

Mr. Semenza, some bishops and pastors want giving to be integrated closely with worship. Some see stewardship to be a key component of spiritual renewal. The concept of stewardship as a gift to God in return for His blessings of time, talent, and treasure appeals to bishops and priests who do not want their people's attention focused entirely on the Church's need for money. However, there is a danger, Mr. Semenza noted, that a rising enthusiasm for stewardship may tempt some fund-raisers and developers to borrow the name without paying the price of building an in-depth theological foundation for their endeavors. If any and every kind of fund-raising is piously called "Christian stewardship," then the whole idea may become badly corrupted. Mr. Semenza admitted, however, that after twenty-five years of promoting stewardship, his organization still has difficulty getting theologians and clerics to do a theology of stewardship related to its doctrinal inspiration and motivation.

Several dioceses such as St. Petersburg, Florida, St. Louis, Missouri, and New Ulm, Minnesota, are deep into stewardship. Monsignor Joseph Champlin, a distinguished liturgist and pastor, has published some widely used parish materials for stewardship.

In the Archdiocese of Chicago, a priests senate committee was appointed in response to Cardinal Joseph Bernardin's request for "alternative fund-raising methods" to replace gambling of all sorts. They are delving into stewardship, possibly to have it integrated with parish planning, a rather successful operation in the archdiocese.

Computer technology undoubtedly will facilitate compilation and inventory of stewardship's "time, talent, and treasure." Some pastors are beginning to see great potential in their parish's multiple resources for much expanded ministries.

Some stewardship, fundamentally rooted in Biblical sources, demands tithing. For example, in the St. Petersburg plan, one percent goes for the diocese, four for the parish, and five for other charities. The St. Louis plan, however, shies away from rigorous tithing, suggesting that "tithing is an obligation that invites challenges we can never answer. Making it voluntary places it where it belongs: one of the many things generous Catholics do--not out of law, but out of love--to deepen their faith."

Figures on the number of people who respond to appeals for full stewardship of their God-given gifts are hard to come by; promoters of stewardship are inclined to let God do the accounting. My impression is that the response is normally small and slow but that "good stewards" do acquire much spiritual benefit from their giving and the financial benefits to the Church range from satisfactory to excellent. Personally, I can see much merit in asking steady, generous contributors to become "stewards"--primarily to give them stewardship's rich spiritual values. I do doubt, however, whether stewardship alone will generate enough income in most dioceses and parishes for the Church to fulfill its obligations in justice to its employees and to its ministries.

Another sign of hope, and the last I will mention, is a recent publication by the National Association of Church Personnel Administrators: *Just*

Treatment for Those Who Work for the Church (not a particularly snappy title). In crisp, clear language, the document sets forth a comprehensive plan for justice to all personnel, avoiding--as far as possible--categories and variables related to clergy, religious, and laity. The plan is tightly summarized in nine ethical principles including affirmative action, compensation, grievances, and termination procedures. Implementation will require radical reforms of present procedures in most diocesan and parish offices, and all of it will cost more money. It will, however, be a great day for the Church when its employees who say, "I work in a Catholic office," can underscore the word "Catholic" because it is completely true.

2.7 / PROTESTANT STEWARDSHIP

Intrigued by the data in the first part of this book which show Protestants doing much better than Roman Catholics in support of their churches, I went searching for an answer to my question "Why?" After looking for a little light in half a dozen books on Protestant stewardship and after discovering that a nearby seminary library had a collection of 1400 volumes on stewardship, I abandoned my plan to go deeply into the topic. (That kind of research would have taken months that I do not have available at this time.) So, I arranged an interview with a gentleman well informed about Protestant stewardship, Reverend Nordan C. Murphy, Executive Director for Stewardship, National Council of the Churches of Christ, headquartered in New York City. Salient points from a three-hour conversation with this genial, affable man of God are these:

Comparison of Protestant and Catholic giving may be quite inaccurate. The Council never has succeeded in obtaining financial reports from all its member churches, and little or nothing from "Protestant" groups that do not belong to the Council or which, though very prosperous, are on the outer edge, if at all, of Protestantism. Rev. Murphy has doubts about the data that are reported; for many churches, bookkeeping is not a high priority. Data that he has seen about Catholic giving seem on the low side, not reflecting donations that Catholics give to religious orders and missionaries or payments that they make for expensive schools.

As with Catholics, so with Protestants-- inflation during the Carter years ran ahead of increased dollar contributions. During the last four years, however, there has been an upsurge in Protestant giving, higher than the slow rate of inflation.

Most of the so-called "mainline" Protestant churches, like urban Roman Catholic churches, have the perplexing problem that twenty percent of the congregation is paying for eighty percent of the expenses.

In Protestant stewardship (and just about everything having to do with funding of Protestant churches is called "stewardship"), the most difficult task is the recruitment and preparation of a sufficient number of volunteer home visitors to solicit pledges. One survey showed that normally only two of three households actually are visited in the course of a parish church's annual stewardship project.

Though Protestant stewardship reaches out to members who come to worship regularly, sporadically, or hardly ever, the best and most consistent response for gifts of time, talent, and treasure (I think Protestants originated that neat alliteration) comes from regular church-goers. Increasingly, Protestant leadership is having doubts about the wisdom of soliciting stewardship from those who see little value in public worship at church.

Not surprisingly, Protestant stewardship emphasizes biblical reasons for making donations. Protestant education, e.g., adult courses and Sunday school, lays out the Old Testament and New Testament foundations for stewardship. Most well-educated Protestants can cite chapters and verses from the Bible as the reasons they fulfill the responsibilities of stewardship. In a Protestant community, plans for improved stewardship begin with a plan for enriched biblical education.

The very essence of Protestant stewardship is a generous, hearty, affective, positive response by a beneficiary of God's goodness and love to this key question: "What shall I render unto the Lord for all He has given to me?" The heart of stewardship is gratitude.

At national and regional meetings on stewardship, much more attention is being focused on a theology of giving--based, of course, on biblical teaching--with less attention on procedures and techniques. Nevertheless, Protestant clergy, like their Roman Catholic brothers of the cloth, are only human; they are all for better theology, but they cannot escape the fact that bills continue to mount in the parish office and *somehow* must be paid. That is where and when stepping around or away from stewardship's ideals becomes a grave temptation.

At the end of our conversation, Reverend Murphy gently remarked, "I long have wondered why Roman Catholics haven't associated their stewardship with the Eucharist. It has surprised me to hear Catholic priests speak about 'taking up a collection' at Mass. In the Roman Catholic tradition, Eucharist is central and celebrated often, several times every Sunday. Giving to the Lord and receiving from the Lord--or the other way around--this reciprocity, this exchange of gifts, is at the heart of the Eucharist."

I gulped and thanked him.

2.8 / CONCLUDING RECOMMENDATIONS

The following recommendations and others in this afterword are compatible with data recorded in the first part of this book. Although most of my recommendations are the same as Father Greeley's, a few are more specific and some are less detailed. Other owe their origin to my forty-eight years of experience in pastoral priesthood, including my years of desk work on behalf of Catholic schools.

1) Catholic leadership, clerical and lay, should ban--or at least call a moratorium on--poor-mouth vocabulary: we can't afford it; Catholics have reached the limit of what they will give to the Church; schools are draining the Church dry; as it is, there is too much emphasis on money; going into debt is crazy; etc.

2) Church administrators and their associates first should assess how much church members have before they decide how much to ask for. Then, the amount which those appealed to will actually give can be calculated.

3) A pivotal point in the U.S. bishops pastoral on the economy is a "preferential option for the poor." This should be specified in a policy that declares that the Church must have a preferential option for its own poor, thousands of its own underpaid employees. This policy should then be put into practice.

4) The NCCB is investing $300,000 in "implementation" of the pastoral letter on the economy. Its purpose is to publicize the letter's teaching. The NCCB should invest at least an equal

amount in setting up specific guidelines and procedures for implementation of the letter's teaching on justice in the Church. Research on this topic might delve into methods to improve cross-funding between dioceses and parishes, use of the Church's vast borrowing potential to finance necessary and desirable ministries (one would think debt is a sin the way the Church avoids it in its financial strategies), analysis of cost-cutting without loss of a ministry's efficaciousness, guidelines for investments, etc.

5) The NCCB Committee on Pastoral Research and Practices, which because of pathetic underfunding and understaffing has virtually stood still since it was started, should move immediately into research on the theology of stewardship and the integration of church support and almsgiving with liturgical worship. Its aim should be to help Catholics make their generous giving a rewarding experience of religious faith. This is a "big money" project and will never come about unless the NCCB completely overhauls the archaic, inefficient, and unjust taxes it levies on dioceses.

6) Twenty years after publication of *The Church in Our Day*--still a powerful and influential ecclesiology for the U.S. Church--the NCCB should undertake an updating of this document. Its ecclesiology is inseparably associated with financing the church's ministries, and it should be clarified with plenty of options. Empirical research in the U.S. Church should not shy away from asking Catholics what they do not like about the Church and why. The purgative way is still a first step toward virtue.

7) Some agency, maybe the NCCB or a Catholic university, should publish a compendium of thousands of "success stories" in dioceses and parishes where the collaboration of clergy and laity has led to full support of post-Vatican II ministries and traditional services. As I see it, the Church's financial condition is not one big mess, but there are some little messes that discredit the Church as a whole. They should be cleaned up quickly.

8) St. Paul, no slouch at fund-raising, wrote: "The Lord loves a cheerful giver." His inspired words prompt me to recommend a mood of cheerful optimism about the Church's future finances. I would not suggest optimism if I feared that Catholics were being financially crippled by their church's extravagant demands or if I suspected that mismanagement of funds was so rotten that Catholics could not in good conscience contribute or if I thought that Catholics were cheapskates who no longer cared about their church or if I felt that the institutional church was doomed and that it was just a matter of time before it disappeared from the American scene. I do not have these fears, suspicions, apprehensions, and nervous feelings. I see it this way: God in His good providence has blessed many U.S. Catholics with wealth that twenty years ago they did not even dream they would have. For the most part, they did not fall into it; they earned it. The years ahead will see increased affluence, and I confidently pray that many of these Catholics will become fascinated by a beautiful concept--"the holy use of money." That is the title of a superb book by Father John C. Haughey, S.J. Some of the first words in his book are an appropriate conclusion to

this one: ". . . in our American culture, money talks all the day long and faith is virtually silent. It's not like faith to be silent, but in the presence of money it has learned to accept a monologue; but there are many reasons why faith needs to talk to money "

Hopefully, Father Greeley's data and our recommendations will suggest some lively topics for a dialogue between faith and money.

NOTE

Camera-ready copy for this report, set in times roman type face, was prepared on a Compaq 386 and a Hewlett-Packard LaserJet[+] printer, using Microsoft Word and Energraphics.

Data analysis was executed with SPSSPC+

Sean Durkin was the research assistant on the project, Mary Kotecki and Helen Horn the typists, Eileen Durkin the editor.